THE
MIND
STRENGTH
PLAYBOOK

MASTER YOUR MIND
ELEVATE YOUR GAME

Maison
Vero

THE
MIND
STRENGTH
PLAYBOOK

MASTER YOUR MIND
ELEVATE YOUR GAME

LUKE FALK

Maison
Vero

Maison
Vero

Published by Maison Vero
3002 Dow Avenue,
Suite 112 Tustin, CA 92780

Maison Vero is a professional publishing house that partners with rising authors to bring their thought leadership to the world. By respecting the copyright of an author's intellectual property, you enable Maison Vero and the author to continue publishing exceptional books for years to come. We thank you for supporting the author's copyright by purchasing an authorized edition of this book.

Inquiries may be directed to: Maison Vero, 3002 Dow Avenue, Suite 112 Tustin, CA 92780, or info@graymilleragency.com.

For information about special discounts for bulk purchases, please call 1-949-333-4872 or email info@graymilleragency.com.

Maison Vero is a partner brand of The Gray + Miller Agency, a speaking, literary, and talent consortium.

For more information on the talent represented by The Gray + Miller Agency, or to bring any of our thought leaders to your organization or live event please visit our website at graymilleragency.com.

Cover Design: Zach Sharples
Layout Design: Mel Wise

Manufactured in the United States of America

ISBN: (paperback) 978-1-9695-0801-1   ISBN: (ebook) 978-1-969508-03-5
ISBN: (hardback) 978-1-969508-02-8

TABLE OF CONTENTS

INTRODUCTION

*"The habits and behaviors you adopt right now
will determine whether you'll face a headwind or
a tailwind in the years and decades to come."*
—Tom Brady

*"The mind governed by the Spirit is life and peace;
the mind governed by the flesh is death."*
—Romans 8:6

Every athlete lives in one of two worlds: Heaven or Hell. Not someday. Not metaphorically. As a lived experience.

It's what happens in the emotional surge of taking the field, putting it on the line, trusting those around you—and trusting yourself. It's what happens when your preparation collides with pressure, and you either rise or unravel.

And if you're a parent or coach watching from the sideline, you've probably felt it too—the pressure, the heartbreak, the hope. You see their highs. You feel their lows. And sometimes, you wish you had a better way to help.

HEAVEN IS REAL. SO IS HELL.

And every athlete knows the difference.

Heaven is the calm in the storm. It's when your body feels light, your instincts take over, and you're locked in—not because the game is easy, but because your mind is clear. Heaven is playing with peace.

Hell is the opposite. It's the tightness in your chest. The hesitation you can't shake. The frustration of knowing you've trained for more but can't access it when it counts. It's the weight of regret. The shame of wasted potential. Hell is playing with fear.

I've lived both.

Some of the greatest highs imaginable as a professional NFL quarterback. And some of the lowest lows—public failure, private pain, and everything in between.

And through it all, I learned this: The difference between Heaven and Hell has almost nothing to do with talent or tactics.

It comes down to mindset.

And more importantly—*Mind Strength*.

WHAT IS MIND STRENGTH?

Mind Strength is the inner ability to respond well when it matters most.

It's what allows you to stay grounded when the pressure hits—to lean into the moment instead of flinching from it. It's the clarity to choose purpose over pressure. The discipline to stay focused when distractions are everywhere. The presence to play with peace—even when everything around you feels chaotic.

It doesn't mean you'll be perfect.

But it does mean you'll be powerful—because you'll be in control of the one thing that matters most: your response.

That's what this book is about.

Not just understanding Mind Strength, but building it. Training it. Owning it. And putting it to work when it counts.

WHO THIS BOOK IS FOR

This book is for athletes—especially those standing at the crossroads of potential and performance.

If you're a competitor who struggles with confidence, consistency, or pressure… If you've got talent but can't seem to play free…

If your thoughts spiral before a big game, or your self-talk turns toxic after a mistake… If you've ever looked in the mirror and thought, "What's wrong with me?"—this book is for you.

And if you're already winning and want that final edge—the margin that separates good from great—this book is for you too.

But it's not just for athletes.

It's also for the coaches who want to build more than just winners on the scoreboard. The ones who understand that leadership starts between the ears.

The ones who care more about who their players become than what stats they put up.

And it's for the parents—especially those watching their sons and daughters ride the emotional rollercoaster of competitive sports.

The ones who see the tears behind the helmet, the self-doubt behind the smile. The ones who want to help—but aren't always sure how.

If any of that describes you, this book will be your roadmap.

You'll gain the tools, language, and perspective to guide the young people you care about—not just to play better, but to live better. To become grounded, gritty, emotionally agile leaders— on and off the field.

WHAT YOU'LL GET

The Mind Strength Playbook is more than stories and inspiration. It's a step-by-step system to build the mental edge that separates good athletes from great ones—and great athletes from elite ones.

Inside, you'll find:

 The Playbook—a repeatable, trainable system of daily mindset practices to build clarity, resilience, and focus.

 Walk-On Wisdom—hard-won lessons from my journey as a college and NFL quarterback, and as a college coach.

 Coaching Tips—proven tools and practical skills to help you grow into the best version of yourself as a coach, and empower your athletes to reach their full potential and gain the winning edge on and off the field.

 Parent Tips—practical guidance to give you a clear roadmap and the answers you need to support your child on their athletic and life journey.

Access to the "*Virtual Locker Room*"—a digital training hub where you'll find bonus tools, guided audios, and support to keep you growing long after you finish reading.

End of Chapter Review—a clear, structured summary that reinforces key teachings and coaching to help you lock in what you've learned and confidently put it into action.

Whether you're reading this on your own, with your team, or as a parent trying to support your athlete from the sidelines, *The Mind Strength Playbook* will show you how to train your mind like you train your body. And learn how to not only win on the scoreboard, but more importantly, in life.

CHAPTER 1

Take Ownership of Your Performance

"There is a choice you have to make, in everything you do.
So keep in mind that in the end, the choice you make,
makes you."

–John Wooden

The Tale of Two Careers

CAREER A

Coming out of high school, I had two options:

The safe route—take my spot at Cornell, a prestigious Ivy League school where I was wanted and football was stable, but it wasn't big-time.

Or the hard route—walk on at Washington State with no guarantees, no scholarship, and a mountain to climb.

At first, I chose safety. I committed to Cornell. But the second I did, I felt a pit in my stomach. I knew I'd made a mistake. I didn't want to live with regrets, always wondering if I could've been a Pac-12 quarterback. Then, almost like confirmation, Cornell's head coach left for the CFL. That was my "green light," as Matthew McConaughey would say. So I picked the harder road.

As a walk-on, I showed up in Pullman with what I call the "Rudy glasses" on—visions of the underdog movie ending, where the crowd chants your name and you get carried off the field.

But the reality? Week 2 of my first season, I fumbled a scout-team snap. My reward? Our linebacker's coach yelling: "#4, get the f*** out of there! I don't want to see your a** in there for another snap!"

The climb was already steep. Now it felt damn near vertical.

"Coach Lose, I don't want to see his a** in there again!" Our linebackers coach continued, hammering the final nail in the coffin for my reps. The rest of the year, I stood behind and watched.

When I first arrived at Washington State, I was fifth string. My incoming class alone had four quarterbacks—two walk-ons and two scholarship players, including a highly touted four-star recruit. He was one of the highest-ranked players the program had landed in recent years, the guy they saw as the foundation for their future.

That first year, nothing came easy. Reps were scarce. Praise was rare. Criticism was constant. I felt like I was more so in the way rather than there to help add any value to the team.

The weight room was brutal for me and a reminder of my place on the team. I was part of the "non-travel" lift—a 6 a.m. "weed out" group designed for fringe players to see who really wanted to stick around. On Friday mornings, we'd finish a heavy squat session, then head straight to the field for the infamous Prowler Sled.

Its warning label stared you straight in the face as you looked down while pushing it:

> "WARNING: USE OF THIS PRODUCT MAY CAUSE PROWLER FLU (VOMITING, NAUSEA, FAINTING, BODY ACHES AND/ OR UPPER RESPIRATORY DISTRESS ASSOCIATED WITH THE ACTIVITY OF PUSHING, PULLING, OR TOWING A PROWLER.)"

That warning wasn't an exaggeration. Guys dropped like flies. Coaches turned it into a race where the last ones to finish were sent to the sideline to do up-downs until the workout ended. The up-downs were easy compared to the sled pushes—it was the hit to your pride, ego, and your place on the depth chart that stung, and as a walk-on, I had no room to spare. As for the four-star? He wasn't there. He got to sleep in.

Off the field, the reminders of my status kept coming. Walk-ons weren't allowed to eat with scholarship players unless they paid extra, so I ate with the regular students. Occasionally, my teammate and buddy Cole Madison snuck me out some mac 'n cheese from the team cafeteria.

Getting books was another gut punch. Scholarship players went straight to the front, grabbed their prepackaged books, and walked out without a bill. I spent thirty minutes scavenging through the bookstore for mine, then stood in line for an hour—like being at Disneyland, except at the end, you forked over $400 instead of getting on a ride.

There were no stipend checks for walk-ons either. No money coming in—just the privilege to pay for the chance to "play." That first summer, I picked up odd jobs to help get some cash in my pocket. One was catering an event for high-ranking university faculty members and staff from the athletic department. I drew the assignment of serving our Athletic Director's table. Rather than being noticed by him and his staff, the only thing that stood out that night was me overhearing their conversation about how they heard the four-star QB was looking great that summer and so on…

Even getting my laundry was a reminder of my rank. Scholarship guys had lockers matching their jersey numbers—up high, easy to reach. Mine? Locker 114, near the floor. Every time I bent over to grab my gear, it was like the program whispering my place to me.

All of this wore on me. Some days, I wondered if I'd made the right call or if I should have taken the opportunity at Cornell where I was wanted. I'd call home and talk through the doubt. But I was met with unwavering support. So I kept going. Kept working.

With this support, I started to take matters into my own hands. I met with coaches to learn the offense. Threw extra routes with teammates after practice.

On off days, I'd lift on my own, then take the script out to the field to walk through plays, practicing the calls and signals like I was under center.

Sure, I didn't have scholarship reps. But I prepared like I did.

All the work started to earn me something that mattered: respect. Even though I wasn't on the field, I was in the weight room, the film room, the practice field, grinding. I built trust with my teammates.

While the four-star rested, I showed up.

Back in my dorm room, I had a vision board that helped keep me locked in. It had two images: one of me earning a scholarship, the other as the starting quarterback. Under each one, I'd written: "I Am earning a full-ride scholarship," and "I Am the starting quarterback for Washington State."

Eventually, the players ahead of me transferred out and Coach Leach was true to his word that he'd give me an opportunity to compete. In spring ball, I found myself going against the four-star QB for the backup job. I outplayed him. That summer, the four-star transferred out too.

Then, heading into fall, a couple of weeks before the 2014 season, Coach Leach pulled me aside after a quarterback meeting.

"You're on scholarship," he said. "Go sign your papers in Emerick's office." Euphoria came over me.

A year earlier, I'd been invisible. Now I was one play away from my dream of being a Pac-12 starter—and no longer paying my own way to chase it.

Later that season, my moment came. Our starting QB went down with an injury in the eighth game against USC. I stepped in.

The next week, I made my first start. Led the team to a win over Oregon State. Got named Pac-12 Player of the Week.

Once again, total euphoria.

To my amazement, I would go on to start 40 games and help lead Washington State to 27 team wins—the most ever by a starting quarterback in school history. Also, being part of Coach Leach's Air Raid system, I was able to throw for 14,486 yards and 119 touchdowns, both Pac-12 records, and was fortunate enough to win the Burlsworth Trophy, awarded to the nation's best player who began as a walk-on, thanks in no small part to the incredible teammates and coaches who made it possible.

None of that was promised.

None of it was easy.

But it all started with one quiet decision—to take ownership of where I was going and find a way.

CAREER B:

"With the 199th pick in the 2018 NFL draft, the Tennessee Titans select… Luke Falk.

QB, Washington State."

Those were the words I had dreamed of hearing since I was a little kid, but they fell flat to me. Instead of feeling excitement, fulfillment, and gratitude for the opportunity, I felt embarrassed, slighted, angry, and entitled.

Now pick 199 is a famous draft spot—it's the number Tom Brady was drafted at in 2000. And where Brady has expressed he felt gratitude and appreciation for getting drafted and having an opportunity, I didn't.

After my junior season, I was projected to be a second- or third-round NFL pick by a number of top-tier agents. I chose not to declare for the draft early and to return for my senior season in pursuit of a Pac-12 championship.

My senior season was rocky, up and down, not the way I had envisioned it going.

I broke my wrist on the third play of our second game vs. Boise State.

I was benched multiple times. I had my lowest career numbers in every statistical category.

Everything seemed to be an uphill battle.

Yet, in my mind, I still held on to those second- or third-round grades for the draft.

So, when draft day finally came, and I didn't hear my name in the second, third, fourth, or fifth round, but in the sixth, I felt hurt, embarrassed, entitled... and rather than seeing the opportunity, I only saw the slight.

I told myself I deserved better.

Then, when I showed up in Nashville on my new team, this victim mindset came with me.

I was third on the depth chart behind two former first-round picks, and thought: *I'll never start—they've already spent the money elsewhere.* Never mind that I had just received a $148,000 signing bonus for simply putting my name on a piece of paper, over a hundred times the amount of my old college stipend, not to mention I was now getting paid to play instead of paying to play like I had as a walk-on.

At practice, I didn't get ignored—I got solid reps, way more than I had as a freshman in college. But I didn't do more than was asked of me. I met occasionally with my quarterback coach. Didn't throw extra with receivers. Didn't walk through the script after practice. Didn't study hard on my own or prioritize recovery. Didn't grind in the weight room. But I did complain. *My wrist isn't right. This offense doesn't fit me. I don't like the coaches.*

Excuses became the norm.

Things outside football weren't much better. My parents were locked in a multiyear divorce that kept spilling into my world. One game, my mom and her brothers sat drunk in the front row, yelling at my coaches. My dad showed up with a new girlfriend. That caused a scene too. It wasn't the first time. Once, after a game, police had to be called.

My engagement wasn't much steadier. The relationship had run its course, but neither wanted to be the one to walk away. So we stayed, stuck in something neither one of us believed in anymore.

Even close relationships faded. My circle thinned. I stopped talking to my sister, one of the closest people in my life, and I isolated myself from those who once grounded me.

This mindset was a far cry from how I started my career at Washington State as a walk-on. Back then, I had so much less, yet I took ownership. I controlled what I could, refused excuses, created a healthy environment for myself, and worked relentlessly. The results spoke for themselves.

But as success came, I stopped working on my Mind Strength, starting in 2017 before my senior season. I let the "Trappings of Success" creep in—entitlement, victimhood, and a "woe is me" attitude. And just like that, the league moved on.

In a year and a half, I bounced between three teams. Started two games. Played in three. And when my chance finally came, I didn't rise to meet it. Instead…

No touchdowns. Three interceptions, one returned for a touchdown. A fumble taken back for six.

After my second start, and my last, I was cut.
Just like that, it was over.

The dream I'd worked my whole life for was gone.

Two Careers, One Choice

Two careers. One life. Same person. Two mindsets. Two very different outcomes.

I've had a lot of time to sit with that contrast—especially since I stepped into coaching. And here's what I've come to believe: My football career didn't fail. It prepared me. Every high, every hard landing. Every moment I took ownership. Every time I didn't. All of it shaped me—not just as a competitor, but as a coach, a mentor, and a man.

It's clear to me now—I wasn't just meant to play football. I was meant to teach it. But more than that, I was meant to coach the *mindset* behind it—the discipline, the belief, and the habits that carry over into everything else.

That is my real calling. So please don't mistake this as the story of someone who missed their potential. It's the story of someone who was being forged for a different purpose, and that's why I'm sharing this with you.

The core principle in this chapter, taking ownership, isn't just the first step of the Mind Strength path. It's the one that holds all the others together. I've lived both sides of it. I've seen what happens when you lean into it and what happens when you don't.

In Career A, I had less—but I owned it. And it led to something great.

In Career B, I had more—but I let go of the mindset that had carried me. I blamed. I drifted. And I lost the opportunity I'd worked my whole life to earn.

Looking back now, I don't see Career B as a failure. I see it as my apprenticeship.

It's what taught me that Mind Strength isn't something you achieve—it's something you maintain. Every day. Or you lose it. It's a journey.

So let's talk about what it means to take ownership—not just in theory, but in practice.

Let's get into the daily habits and mental shifts that build a foundation for everything else in this playbook. Because once you take ownership, everything else becomes possible.

OWNERSHIP STRATEGIES

Here's how to own your performance:

- Change Your Thinking
- Control the Controllable
- Use Your Breath
- Employ E + P + R = O
  (Event + *Perception* + Reaction = Outcome)
- Practice Daily Gratitude for What You Have

Change Your Thinking

People who take ownership of their lives look for and find solutions while the victim-minded person looks for and finds excuses.

Has something unfair ever happened to you? A family crisis? A coach who didn't believe in you? An injury at the worst possible time? A teacher who played favorites? A situation where you got judged not for what you did, but for who you were or where you came from?

Every room I've ever spoken in—whether a locker room, a classroom, or a boardroom—every hand goes up when I ask that question.

Mine included.

Life doesn't play favorites. It doesn't care if you're rich or broke, White or Black, talented or struggling. Eventually, everyone gets hit with something they didn't deserve. But here's the real difference maker: how you respond. You can't always control what happens to you, but you can always control how you think about it. You can decide to be a victim or own it—either way, the choice is yours.

TWO MINDSETS, TWO PATHS

Let's break this down. Here's what it looks like in real life—using my own football career.

Victim Thinking (Career B—My NFL Years)

1. They blame their circumstances.
"I was a late-round draft pick."
"My wrist wasn't fully healed."
"This offense doesn't fit me."

2. They blame other people.

"Coach Leach killed my draft stock by benching me."
"My parents weren't around when I needed to decide about the NFL."
"My agent didn't do enough to help me out."

3. They make excuses.

"The NFL is political—they only give real chances to high draft picks."
"My O-line wasn't strong."
"We had to play all the playoff teams on the road."
"How can I focus with all this stuff going on at home?"

4. They believe life isn't fair.

"Why is this happening to me?"
"I always catch the bad breaks."

5. They act entitled.

"I had a great college career—why didn't I go higher in the draft?"
"I was supposed to be a second- or third-round pick."

This thinking traps you. When everything's someone else's fault, you've handed over all your power. You're stuck waiting on the world to change instead of changing yourself.

It's like being Eeyore from Winnie the Pooh—constantly moping, constantly defeated. As Dave Ramsey puts it, these are the folks whose life motto is: "Woe is me." You see it in politics all the time—endless blame, no solutions. Is it any wonder why progress feels impossible?

Ownership Thinking (Career A—My Early College Years)

Now contrast that with a different mindset—the one I had during my early college years and what I call Ownership Thinking. It looks like this:

1. **They believe they can improve their situation.**

"I don't like where I'm at—but I can do something about it."

2. **They own everything.**

"I overslept. That's on me. I'll fix it tomorrow."

3. **They earn everything and feel entitled to nothing.**

"No one owes me a thing. I've got to earn it—every rep, every play, every shot."

4. **They look for solutions instead of excuses.**

"What's in my control right now? Let's start there."

👟 WALK-ON WISDOM

NOBODY WANTS A VICTIM-MINDED PERSON ON THEIR TEAM

It's January 2018, and I'm in Mobile, Alabama, for the Senior Bowl. My agent had arranged a "mock interview" with the Chicago Bears to help me prepare for meetings with other NFL teams that week and for the upcoming NFL Combine.

I walk into the room—it feels like the entire Bears organization is there, from the head coach on down. They put me through the wringer. I leave thinking I crushed it.

Later, I call my agent. He'd asked a friend who was part of the Bears organization and was in the room to give us some honest feedback. The response?

"They didn't like the interview. They thought you threw Coach Leach under the bus too much."

What they could have said was this: *"They didn't like your victim mindset."*

Even if they had said it that bluntly, I probably still wouldn't have listened. The story and reality I had created was that

Coach Leach, and the rift between us in my last year, caused my poor play.

Oh, how naive I was. I didn't look in the mirror. I didn't see that the person I needed to point the finger at wasn't Coach Leach… It was me.

I didn't get this lesson until I was forced to hang up my cleats. I didn't realize how deep I'd sunk into that victim mindset. And it stunk. I carried it with me into every team, every situation, every opportunity that came after.

Here's the truth: Nobody wants to draft a victim. Nobody wants to recruit one, hire one, date one, or partner with one.

If you want to build real Mind Strength, start here: **Own it all.**

Own your path. Own your progress. Own your highs and your lows.

If a game doesn't go your way, resist the urge to point the finger. Instead, ask: *What's within my control? What can I do better?*

Make this mindset your foundation, and you'll be amazed at how far you can go—not just in sports, but in life.

🐚 COACHING TIP

YOU ARE EITHER COACHING IT OR ALLOWING IT TO HAPPEN

"You are either coaching it or allowing it to happen."

That sign hung in Coach Leach's office. In every assistant's office. In every meeting room. It wasn't décor, but a daily reminder: Take ownership.

As a leader, this mindset is *everything*. When you accept responsibility, you gain the ability to grow and improve. You start looking for ways to get your message across better, get better buy-in and follow-through. You become part of the solution.

But when you fall into victim thinking—blaming your players, your job, your circumstances—you give your power away. You become reactive instead of effective.

This is the core concept of being a great coach and leader: Accept the responsibility and ownership that comes with the position.

Pro Tip: Adopt this mindset fully. You are responsible for what happens within your team, your organization, and your culture. You are coaching or allowing it to happen.

You are both the problem and the solution. The choice is up to you and how you choose to respond. Accept responsibility and you reclaim your power to lead and create positive change. Deflect, blame, and complain? You and your team will remain bound.

(PHOTO CREDIT: WSU FOOTBALL EQUIPMENT)

So how do we take ownership instead of falling into victim thinking? Here are some foundational tools to help you do it:

Control the Controllable

*"If you get caught up in things over which you have no control,
it will adversely affect those things over which you have control."*
–John Wooden

Try this:

Make the weather change.

Grow 2 inches taller.

Get the President of the United States to say something you want him to say—today.

How'd that go?

You didn't even try, did you? Of course not. Those things are silly, impossible, a waste of energy. They're completely outside your control.

And yet, we do this to ourselves all the time.

We obsess over what other people think. We worry about whether a coach will give us playing time. We stress about our ranking, our opponent, the playoff bracket, or a comment somebody made about us online. We fixate on something we can't change—our genetics, our past mistakes, our family situation—and we burn mental fuel wishing it were different.

WHAT HAPPENS WHEN YOU FOCUS ON WHAT YOU CAN'T CONTROL

There are two guaranteed outcomes when you focus on what's out of your hands:

1. You waste time and energy.

Your attention is your most valuable resource. Every moment you spend thinking about things you can't control is a moment you aren't improving, preparing, or performing. It's like trying to run a race with a parachute strapped to your back. It's the biggest waste of time and energy you can make as an athlete—or a human being.

2. Your anxiety skyrockets.

This one is detrimental—not just to your performance, but to the quality of your life.

Dr. Craig Manning, my old sports psychologist, taught me this: When you focus on things you can't control, your anxiety increases.

Why? Because your brain senses a threat it can't neutralize. You've handed the steering wheel of your emotional state to someone—or something—else.

And when anxiety goes up, performance goes down. So does your quality of life. Let me give you an example we probably all have experienced.

BACKSEAT DRIVERS

Have you ever experienced a backseat driver—barking orders at you, frantic, and audibly anxious?

Why does this happen?

Because they're not in control. They're not the one behind the wheel.

And when they're focused on not being in control, their anxiety goes up and the quality of their ride goes down.

Now, compare that to the driver. No frantic shouting. No spike in anxiety. Why? Because they're the one controlling the wheel.

This same dynamic plays out for athletes. The ones who obsess over what the fans will say, what the media will write, whether the coach will play them, the outcome of the game, or the future—

are focusing on things they can't control. By doing that, they voluntarily raise their anxiety, and in turn, their performance plummets and they don't enjoy the *"ride."*

That's how it works:

- Focus on what you can't control $\rightarrow$ anxiety goes up.
- Focus on what you can control $\rightarrow$ anxiety goes down.

And when anxiety goes down?

Performance goes up.

Quality of life goes up.

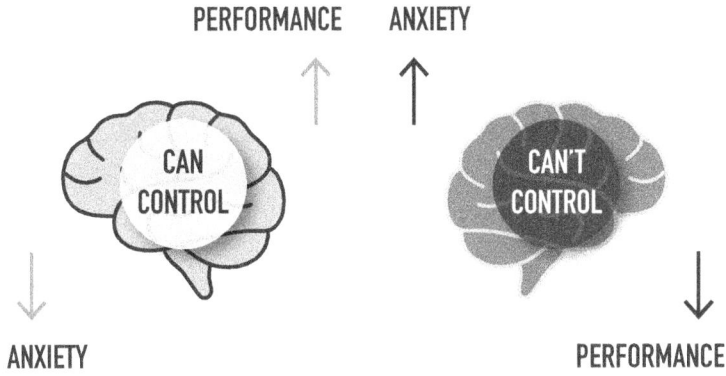

Here's the mindset shift:

- You can't control what others say, think, or do.
- You can't control the past or predict the future.
- But you can control your effort. Your focus. Your preparation. Your response.

Master the Inner World:
Why Control Starts From the Inside Out

The biggest difference between what you can control and what you can't comes down to this:

What you can control is INTERNAL.

What you can't control is EXTERNAL.

Let's break that down.

Things You Can Control (Internal)	*Things You Can't Control (External)*
• Your thoughts	• What others say or do
• Your attitude	• Whether a coach plays you
• Your effort	• Who colleges recruit
• Your perception	• The outcome of a game
• Your breathing	• Media coverage
• Your response	• The weather
• Your work ethic	• Social media comments
• Your preparation	• What people think of you
• Your habits	• The past
• Your integrity	• The future
• Your mindset	
• The present moment	

This distinction is foundational. Why? Because **Mind Strength training is about mastering your inner world so that you can handle anything the external world throws at you.** This approach—working from the inside out—isn't just good advice. It's essential. As Stephen R. Covey put it in *The 7 Habits of Highly Effective People*, true effectiveness always begins with internal mastery, not external manipulation.

You can't control the world. You can only control your choices in it.

And that's the ground we build on in this program. Every tool we give you, every strategy we practice—it all comes back to that one aim: strengthening your internal control system. Not trying to manipulate the external noise.

THE TURNAROUND: CHOOSE TO REFOCUS

So if you're dealing with performance anxiety, or just life anxiety, check where your focus is. Chances are, it's on something outside your control.

The antidote? A decision. Make one simple choice to shift your attention to something *you can control*. Your breathing. Your attitude. Your next rep. Your prep for tomorrow.

So the next time your mind drifts toward worry, regret, or frustration, ask yourself: "Is this in my control?"

If the answer is no, let it go. Then quickly move toward what is, because that's where your power lives.

One of the greatest tools I use to refocus on what I can control is my breath. It's simple, always accessible, and incredibly powerful.

And here's the truth: It can anchor you too—anytime, anywhere.

Let's dive into it.

Use Your Breath

"Feelings come and go like clouds in a windy sky. Conscious breathing is my anchor." –Thich Nhat Hanh

Your breath is a superpower—if you learn to use it.

It's also one of the clearest signals of what state your mind and body are in. Think about it:

- When you're nervous, your breath becomes shallow, fast, and high in the chest.
- When you're calm or asleep, your breath is slow, deep, and low in the belly.

This isn't random; it's hard-wired. Your breath links directly to your autonomic nervous system, which controls your fight-or-flight (sympathetic) and rest-and-digest (parasympathetic) responses. Shallow, rapid breathing triggers stress. Deep, diaphragmatic breathing activates calm.

In other words, your breath isn't just a response—it's a steering wheel.

And it's not just mental.

In sports physiology, regulated breathing has been shown to improve focus, heart rate variability (HRV), emotional regulation, and even reaction time[1]—all critical to peak performance. So if you're stepping into a big game, a tough practice, or even a hard conversation, and you feel your heart racing—stop just waiting to calm down. Use your breath to calm down.

4-6 Breathing

This is one of the simplest and most effective tools I use with clients and for myself. It's called 4-6 breathing. Here's how it works:

Breathe in through your nose for 4 seconds, then breathe out through your nose for 6 seconds.

That's it.

Why nose breathing? Because it slows you down and keeps your breath controlled. When athletes try to breathe through their mouth, especially under pressure, they often overbreathe, taking in too much air or letting too much out, and end up gasping when they need to stay steady. Nose breathing builds control.

This simple breathing pattern has three major benefits. First, it brings your attention back to something you can control. That alone reduces anxiety. Second, when you're focused on counting your breath, "1, 2, 3, 4…" you're not stuck in the future or replaying the past. You're present. And third, deep breathing sends a simple message to your body: You're safe. That signal drops your heart rate, steadies your nerves, and helps you perform from a calm, locked-in place—not a frantic one.

But like any skill, this only works if you train it. You wouldn't show up to a tournament without practicing your swing or your shot. Same with breathwork. If you wait until game time to try this for the first time, you won't be able to access it when you need it most.

THE PLAYBOOK

THE 4–6 BREATHING METHOD

Your breath is your reset button. Use it. Train it. Trust it.

Start small—one minute a day—before practice, after workouts, and in bed at night.

Build the habit now, so when the pressure hits, your body knows exactly what to do.

1. Place a hand on your belly.

2. Inhale for 4 seconds—feel your belly rise.

3. Exhale for 6 seconds—feel your belly fall.

That feeling of your belly rising and falling is how you know you're using your diaphragm—not your chest. Chest breathing is shallow and panicked. Belly breathing is deep and calm.

COACHING TIP

APPLYING THE 4-6 BREATHING METHOD

Breathwork is one of the fastest ways to help your athletes manage stress, stay present, and regulate their nervous system. But like any skill, it has to be trained before it's needed.

The 4-6 breathing method is simple and effective:

Inhale through the nose for 4 seconds. Exhale through the nose for 6 seconds. To help athletes build this into their routine, I recommend two strategies:

1. **Start small and scale.**

Have your athletes begin with just 1 minute per day. Once they've done that consistently for a week, bump it up to 2 minutes. Add a minute per week until they reach 5 minutes. That progression builds muscle memory and buy-in without feeling overwhelming.

2. **Use habit stacking.**

From James Clear's bestselling book *Atomic Habits*, the easiest way to build a new habit is to attach it to an existing one. Have athletes stack 4-6 breathing onto routines they already do—like brushing their teeth, driving to school, tying their cleats, or lying down at night.

For example: *"After you brush your teeth in the morning, spend 1 minute on 4-6 breathing."* This kind of cue-based repetition helps make breathwork automatic and accessible in pressure moments.

Bottom line: Avoid just telling athletes to "breathe"—teach them to train it. And help them build it into their day before they need it on the field or court.

PARENT TIP

APPLYING THE 4-6 BREATHING METHOD

This isn't just a performance tool for athletes; it's a life skill you can use too.

I remember one night around midnight, my daughter woke my wife and me with violent vomiting. It went on for hours. Eventually, we made the call to take her to the ER. On the drive over, I could feel the tension in my body—tight muscles, a knot in my stomach, short, shallow breathing.

My mind spiraled toward everything I couldn't control:

What if something's seriously wrong? Will they figure it out? What happens next? Then I caught myself.

At that moment, I knew exactly what I needed to do. I turned my attention to my breath and started using the 4-6 method: inhale for 4 seconds, exhale for 6, all through the nose. Within a few minutes, my body relaxed. My heart rate dropped. My thoughts slowed down. I was back in the present—and in a better headspace to support my daughter and make clear, rational decisions.

Here's the truth: If I hadn't practiced this skill ahead of time, I wouldn't have had access to it when I needed it most. That's how breathwork works—you don't rise to the level of your intention; you fall to the level of your preparation.

To make it easier to build this habit, we've included a guided audio session in your "*Virtual Locker Room*." You can listen to it anytime. I found that having someone walk me through the breathing pattern, especially in the beginning, helped me stay consistent and actually do it.

 Use the QR code to take the first step. This might become one of the most reliable tools you have—not just in high-pressure moments, but in everyday parenting too.

Employ E + P + R = O

(EVENT + *PERCEPTION* + RESPONSE = OUTCOME)

"No matter what happens in the external world, you ALWAYS have control of your inner world." –Wayne Dyer

There's a formula a lot of coaches and sports psychologists use. Urban Meyer made it famous: E + R = O. That stands for Event + Response = Outcome.

I used it for years with athletes and teams. It's solid. But in my experience, it's missing one thing—something that comes before Response…

"*P*," which stands for **Perception**.

So here's the full version I teach now:

E + P + R = O.

Event + *Perception* + Response = Outcome.

Why add "*P*"? Because how you perceive an event shapes the entire chain. Your perception is the story you tell yourself—the meaning you assign to what just happened. And that story determines how you respond.

Let's break this down:

- **E (Event):** Outside your control. Injury, coaching decision, bad call.
- *P* (*Perception*): Fully within your control. The story you create.
- **R (Response):** Also in your control. Your behavior, emotion, focus.
- **O (Outcome):** Influenced heavily by your P + R, even though you don't control it directly.

TWO KINDS OF STORIES

When something hard happens, you always write a story in your mind. And typically, it falls into one of two categories:

- Empowering stories: "This will make me better."
- Disempowering stories: "This always happens to me."

These stories may seem like thoughts, but what they really are is perception. And your perception is powerful, as it becomes the filter through which you see the event—and the launchpad for your response. The key is to learn to change your perception, and your response changes with it.

But here's the challenge: Your brain is wired to default to the negative story.

That's not weakness, it's biology.

In psychology, there's a concept called the fundamental attribution error.[2] It's our brain's built-in bias to explain other people's behavior based on their character.

"He's lazy."

"She doesn't care."

"They're just not committed."

But when we judge ourselves, we tend to blame the situation, not our character, for our behavior.

"I was tired."

"Coach didn't explain it right."

"The ref blew the call."

"I had too much going on."

Combine that with *negativity bias*[3]—our tendency to pay more attention to threats than opportunities—and you can see why your brain often spins events into victim-minded, worst-case stories before you've even had a chance to think about it.

As psychologist Roy Baumeister and his team wrote in a foundational paper, "Bad is stronger than good." Our minds naturally overfocus on negative stimuli—by a ratio of about 5:1—because that helped us survive when threats were everywhere. But what kept us alive on the savanna can sabotage us on the field or in the locker room.[4]

If you don't train your perception, your default will be:

"This always happens to me."

"Why does nothing ever go my way?"

"I'll never get a shot."

And once that story gets written, it drives your response. That's why this chapter, and this playbook, puts so much weight on *"P"* in the formula.

Perception isn't a soft skill. It's a performance skill. When you learn to recognize the story you're telling yourself and flip it into something empowering, everything else starts to follow—your focus, your composure, your decisions, and your outcomes.

MY TWO CAREERS—SAME EVENTS, DIFFERENT OUTCOMES

You saw this play out in my own story.

In college, the events were rough. I was a walk-on. Fifth string. No reps. No scholarship. But I chose to view that situation as fuel. I told myself: *This is where I earn it.* That perception led to a strong response—extra work, leadership, discipline—which shaped the outcome: success, records, the starting job.

In the NFL, I had more resources, more opportunity, but my perception shifted. I saw every challenge as a slight, every setback as unfair. I stopped owning it. And that perception triggered weak responses—excuses, blame, disengagement. The outcome? I underperformed, lost the opportunity, and "victimized" my way right out of the NFL.

THE TWINS

A coach once shared a story with me that hit hard—and stuck.

Two twin brothers grew up as orphans. Same DNA. Same home. Same early adversity. As adults, their lives couldn't have looked more different. One built a life marked by purpose and stability—a strong family, a steady career, solid health. The other floundered—no job, no real relationships, chronic health issues, no sense of direction.

A journalist found out and asked the same question to each of them: "How did this happen?"

The first brother said, "**I was an orphan.** I had to make something of myself. I didn't want to repeat the past."

The second brother said, "**I was an orphan.** What chance did I have?"

Same event. Same circumstances. Same initial answer. Different perceptions. Different responses. Different outcomes. That's E + P + R = O in real life.

👟 WALK-ON WISDOM

YOUR CURRENT CIRCUMSTANCES ARE PREPARING YOU

In the 2011 Utah High School State Championship Game, my school, Logan High, sealed a perfect 14-0 season with a game-winning touchdown at Rice-Eccles Stadium. It was a moment for the ages—one of the greatest high school teams in Utah history.

But I wasn't on the field. I wasn't even on the sideline. I was up in the stands—behind the camera, filming it all.

At the end of 2010, my family had moved to California halfway through my sophomore year. A year later, the move fell apart, and we came back a few games into that 2011 season. But by then, I'd been ruled ineligible under Utah's transfer rules—and my old team was rolling without me.

I couldn't practice. I couldn't suit up. I couldn't even be on the field. To say that year was hard is an understatement.

But instead of letting me sulk, my high school coach, Mike Favero, gave me a different role.

He made me a GA (Graduate Assistant). I was tasked with filming games, breaking down tape, and doing the behind-the-scenes work nobody sees.

While the team chased perfection on the field, I was chasing growth off it.

It was agonizing to watch from the press box, behind the camera, as DJ Nelson—one of the state's all-time great high school QBs—sealed the perfect season with a game-winning touchdown pass. But looking back now, that year shaped me.

That's where I learned how to study film.

That's where I developed a real work ethic. That's where I found my competitive edge.

That's where I laid the foundation for my Mind Strength—the preparation, discipline, and humility that helped me become a record-breaking quarterback.

Fast-forward six years, November 2017. I'm back at Rice-Eccles Stadium.

But this time, I'm not filming. This time, I'm playing against the University of Utah. Third and Goal. I audibled: "Easy, Easy! 617!"

Touchdown to Kyle Sweet. My 117th career TD. A new Pac-12 record.

Same stadium. Very different role.

So wherever you are right now, maybe you feel stuck, overlooked, facing an injury, not the starter, suspended, or like life just didn't go as planned, ask yourself:

Are you going to complain… or are you going to grow?

Because that role or circumstance you didn't want… might be the exact training you need.

Be great where you're at.

Everything is preparation for your highest purpose—
if you choose to perceive it that way.

Stay ready. Your moment is coming.

(PHOTO CREDIT: BKT IMAGES)

Description: The 2011 Logan High Football Team celebrating at Rice-Eccles Stadium after sealing a perfect 14-0 season with a State Championship victory, while my teammates stormed the field. I was behind the camera, filming it all—capturing history from the other side of the lens.

(PHOTO CREDIT: SPOKESMAN-REVIEW)

Description: In 2017 at Rice-Eccles Stadium against the University of Utah, I broke the Pac-12 all-time passing record—coming full circle on the same field where I once stood behind a camera, filming my high school team's state championship.

⤵ THE PLAYBOOK

FLIP THE STORY

You can't always control what happens. But you can always control the story you write about it.

This drill helps you catch disempowering thoughts early and flip them into something that actually helps you take action. If you train this skill consistently, it becomes second nature—especially in the heat of competition.

Step 1: Name the Event (E)

Think of something that didn't go your way. A mistake. A benching. A loss. A conversation that rattled you. Write it down.

Example: *"Coach didn't put me in during the fourth quarter."*

Step 2: Name the Story (P)

Now be honest. What story did your mind start telling you in that moment?

Example: *"He doesn't believe in me."*

"I'll never earn his trust." "

I blew my shot."

That story is your perception—and it's shaping everything that comes next.

Step 3: Flip the Story

Now flip it. Rewrite the story in a way that empowers you to move forward. Focus on what you can control.

Example: *"He made a decision. I can learn from it, respond well, and earn the next opportunity."*

Step 4: Choose Your Response (R)

Now write down your next move—something specific, within your control, that puts you back in the driver's seat.

Example: *"I'll ask for film review and show up early to the next team session."*

This is how you rewire your perception. One story at a time. One decision at a time.

And over time? You change your outcomes.

COACHING TIP

TRAIN THE PERCEPTION FLIP

Your athletes don't respond to events—they respond to the story they tell themselves about those events.

That's why training perception is just as critical as training physical reps. If an athlete spins a disempowering story— "Coach doesn't believe in me," "I always screw up," "This isn't fair"—their response will reflect it. Poor perception leads to poor performance.

That's where the Perception Flip comes in.

Here are some ideas for implementing this into your coaching routine:

1. Build the habit during non-game moments.

Avoid waiting for a high-pressure failure. After a tough rep in practice, pull them aside and say:

"What story did you just tell yourself?"
"How would you flip it into something useful?"

2. Make the formula visible.

Put $E + P + R = O$ on the whiteboard. On the locker room door. In the film room. When athletes see it consistently, they'll start recognizing when they're slipping into bad perception.

3. Celebrate good flips.

When an athlete rewrites a negative story and shows maturity in their response, call it out. Reinforce the win: *"That's a great flip. That's what leaders do."*

4. Use language cues.

Athletes often leak perception in how they speak. Train them to catch phrases like:

"I always…" "They never…" "Why me?"

These are red flags. Redirect with:

"What's one thing in your control?" "What's a more useful story right now?"

Bottom line: If you want tougher athletes, stop just telling them to respond better. Teach them to see better first. Because the story they choose drives the future they create.

PARENT TIP

WHAT STORY ARE YOU TELLING YOURSELF?

"Luke, what story are you making up about this?"

That was a question my dad asked me growing up whenever I faced a tough situation. He helped me see that it wasn't the event itself that held the power—it was the story I told myself about it. Even today, if I call him about a challenge I'm facing, he'll say the same thing: *"What story are you telling yourself?"*

As a parent, you can do the same. When your child comes to you with something hard, ask them:

"What story are you telling yourself about this?"

Then help them flip it together and create an empowering one.

It won't just make them better athletes, it will make them stronger thinkers and more resilient people.

Practice Daily Gratitude for What You Have

Gratitude is a guardrail that keeps your mind from sliding down the slippery slope of victim thinking.

When your focus shifts to what you lack—what's missing, unfair, or out of reach—it doesn't take long for the victim mindset to creep in. It's subtle at first. You start noticing what others have. What you don't. The things you think you should've earned by now. Before long, you're stuck seeing your life through a glass-half-empty, or maybe totally-empty, lens.

But when you focus on what you do have, when you practice gratitude, you reclaim control of the narrative. You shift the lens. You remind yourself what's right in your world. That's not just a feel-good exercise. It's a powerful antidote to victim thinking.

I lived both sides of this.

In college, I didn't have a scholarship, a spot on the depth chart, or any guarantees. But I was grateful for the opportunity to compete. I was paying my way to chase a dream—and that gratitude fueled ownership. It made me focus on what I could control. It gave me energy to work when nobody was watching. And that mindset changed the outcome.

But when I got to the NFL, that lens flipped. Instead of being grateful to be drafted, I felt embarrassed that I'd slid to the sixth round. That disappointment planted a seed—a disempowering one. And instead of weeding it out, I let it grow. I saw myself as slighted. Undervalued.

That was the beginning of the mindset drift—and I didn't course-correct in time.

So I'll ask you: *What are you taking for granted?*

Is it your spot on the team? Your relationships? Your health?

Are you spending your energy wishing for more—more status, more playing time, someone else's talent—while missing what's already in your hands?

The biggest example? Health.

Every time I get sick, even just a cold, I remember how much I took feeling strong for granted. How many days did I wake up with energy, a clear mind, and no pain… and never said a word of thanks? That kind of awareness? It changes things.

And if we were more intentional about thanking God for our blessings—especially the ones we forget to notice—our quality of life would improve dramatically. Gratitude anchors you in ownership. It reminds you that even if you don't control everything, you still have so much you can build from.

Now, I want to be clear on this: Gratitude isn't about lowering your ambition. It's about lifting your perspective. You can pursue more and still be thankful for what's here now. You can strive for better and still honor where you've come from.

One phrase I came up with that helps me keep this mindset sharp is: **"Water the grass beneath your feet as you continue to move toward your goals and dreams."**

It means being deeply grateful for where you are—while staying committed to where you're going.

⌕ THE PLAYBOOK

DAILY GRATITUDE RESET

Right after your breathwork, when your body is calm and your mind is centered, take 30 seconds to practice gratitude.

Step 1: Name three things you're grateful for.

Keep it simple. It could be your health, your family, your team, your ability to move and compete. Whatever's true in that moment.

Step 2: Breathe them in.

As you inhale, mentally focus on one of those things. As you exhale, let that sense of gratitude settle deeper.

Step 3: Repeat for each one.

Three full breath cycles. That's it.

This exercise isn't just about feeling good. It's about training your perception.

Gratitude grounds you in what's real and right in your life. It replaces scarcity with perspective. It takes your focus off what's missing and puts it on what you can build from.

It's why elite coaches like Tony Robbins make this a daily discipline—it doesn't just change your attitude, it changes your response. And when your response improves, so does your outcome.

Gratitude doesn't just lift your mood, it enhances your Mind Strength.

Chapter 1 Review—Take Ownership

"Things turn out best for those who make the best of the way things turn out." –John Wooden

To close this chapter, there's a quote I often use in my coaching sessions. I call it "The GOAT Quote." It's from Tom Brady referencing his TB12 Method in a Facebook quote, and I think it perfectly captures what this entire chapter has been about:

"...If, like me, you're serious about your peak performance, you need to work hard at the things that are within your control: your work ethic, how you treat your body, and your attitude. Especially your attitude. Things happen sometimes that I don't welcome or want, but I make the choice to remain positive. That is something within my control. I don't like to focus on negatives or to make excuses. I am never a victim. I gain nothing if I get angry or frustrated. You can make life a lot harder for yourself by focusing on negative things in your path or making excuses for why things didn't go your way. Or, you can refuse to take things personally, let them go, learn from them, and become the best version of yourself. It's a choice. It's actually your choice. If I throw an interception or have a bad day or make a bad business decision, by staying in that place I will just make things worse. Wisdom, someone said, is about knowing the difference between the things you can control and the things you can't."[5]

That's it. That's taking ownership.

As Brady says, and as I've lived, you can use what happens to you to get stronger, or you can use it to make excuses. But either way, it's a choice.

That's the heart of Mind Strength. We've covered a lot in this first chapter:

- The difference between victim thinking and Ownership Thinking.
- How to control the controllable.
- The power of breathwork, perception, and gratitude.
- The mindset model of E + P + R = O.
- And most importantly, how to apply all of it—daily, practically, and intentionally.

But none of it matters if it just stays on the page. This chapter wasn't written to inspire you. It was written to invite you—to challenge you—to decide. Because this journey starts and ends with a question only you can answer:

Will you own your story—or will you let your story own you?

You don't have to be perfect. You don't have to have all the answers.

You just have to start by taking ownership of what's in your hands right now. That's the first step.

And if you take it—everything else becomes possible.

CHAPTER 2

Overcome an Athlete's Biggest Hurdle:
Needing Approval

"Needing approval is tantamount to saying,
'Your view of me is more important
than my own opinion of myself.'"

–Wayne Dyer

Choking at the Apple Cup

It's late November, and I'm stepping onto the field at Husky Stadium for the 2017 Apple Cup—the final game of the regular season against our cross-state rival, the University of Washington. The stakes couldn't have been higher. A win would propel us to the Pac-12 Championship game and a chance to play in the Rose Bowl, one of the most prestigious bowl games in college football. Personally, this game was also pivotal for my future—the NFL draft was looming, and a standout performance could significantly improve my prospects.

The stadium was electric, packed with fans clad in purple and crimson, their cheers battling each other through the chilly Seattle drizzle. Every breath felt sharp, mixing adrenaline with the cold, damp air. My heart pounded heavily beneath my pads, each beat echoing louder as I took the first snap.

But when it mattered most—I choked. My throws sailed errantly; decisions came slowly, muddled by anxiety. Each mistake intensified the next, spiraling into one of my worst performances ever on this grand stage. I was paralyzed by the fear of disappointing my teammates, coaches, family, and the thousands watching. What should have been a moment of triumph turned into overwhelming embarrassment.

Why did I choke? Because I didn't just want approval—I *needed* it. And that made all the difference.

(PHOTO CREDIT: GREG & ASHLEY DAVIS)

THE HUMAN NEED FOR APPROVAL

I know I'm not alone. Many of you reading this have either experienced a moment where you choked under pressure or dread finding yourself in that situation. Why does choking happen? Why did it happen to me at this critical time, despite countless other times when I delivered in clutch situations? The answer is clear: My *need* for approval overtook my mental discipline.

We're social creatures. We naturally desire approval. We love to hear "good job" from our parents, teachers, coaches, and peers. We want to fit in and feel accepted. Research has shown time and again how powerfully we are driven by this need for acceptance and the extraordinary lengths we'll go to achieve it.

Wanting approval isn't inherently bad. In fact, I'm writing this book hoping you'll approve, hoping you'll find value in it. But when this desire becomes a *need*—when our self-worth hinges on someone else's opinion—that's when we're in trouble. That's when we fall into what I call the "Teeter-Totter Trap."

I've been there. Many athletes, coaches, and high performers I've coached have been there too. "Approval seekers" derive their self-worth externally, from the opinions of parents, coaches, peers, fans, or media. When we receive approval, we soar. When approval is withheld, we crash. Our emotional state rides the highs and lows of external validation, much like a teeter-totter controlled by someone else.

Approval seekers typically get validation through two main avenues:

Outcome: Performing well and achieving positive outcomes earns approval (teeter-totter goes up).

Comparison: Comparing ourselves to others and feeling superior provides validation (teeter-totter goes up). Conversely, falling short means losing approval (teeter-totter goes down).

Most playgrounds are fun, but this one is dangerous. It's a vicious cycle, trapping participants in what feels like a mental prison.

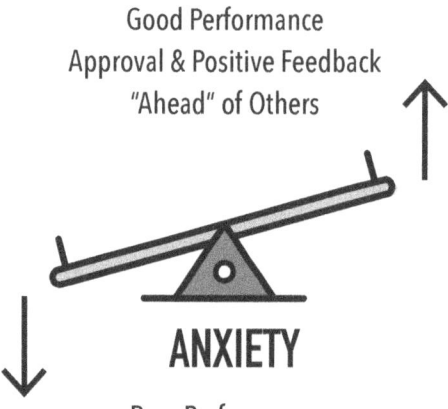

Good Performance
Approval & Positive Feedback
"Ahead" of Others

ANXIETY

Poor Performance
No Approval & Negative Feedback
"Behind" Others

High achievers often fall into this trap early, seeking love or acceptance they didn't fully receive in childhood. They chase achievement, believing it will finally deliver the love they crave.

This was my experience growing up. In my household, performance was everything.

After a good game, things at home were great—I felt worthy and loved. But after a poor performance, the atmosphere turned tense, critical. I remember vividly being 11 years old, cornered in my bathroom, my mom frantically shouting, "What's wrong with you? Why can't you be more aggressive like your Uncle Jeff?" (Jeff was a celebrated athlete, the top high school athlete in Utah, who later played basketball at Utah State.)

The message I internalized was: "Perform well, and you're valuable, you're loved. Fail, and you're not." Love felt conditional. I know my parents loved me deeply, and I'm not here to criticize my upbringing. Those experiences shaped me profoundly, enabling me now to help many young people and athletes break free from this painful cycle. Often parents who pressure their kids like this are the very ones who eventually seek my coaching for their children. What an opportunity to pay it forward, helping these young people escape the trap.

The mechanics behind this approval seeking are simple yet damaging. When we rely on outcomes and comparisons for approval, we focus on things outside our control. Anxiety rises, and performance and overall quality of life decrease. Let's talk specifically about the outcome.

Can you truly control the outcome of your performance? Many athletes and coaches initially argue that they can. But when you dig deeper, you realize outcomes—especially in team sports—involve many uncontrollable factors: your opponent, weather, coaches' decisions, referees, and teammates' performances. When your identity and self-worth depend on the outcome, anxiety skyrockets and performance plummets—especially under pressure. This scenario creates the perfect conditions for choking.

Performance-Approval Strategies

The good news is, you can prevent choking and deliver in the clutch. In this chapter, I'll introduce you to four practical tools to shift from being approval seeking to becoming more self-secure.

APPROVAL SEEKING	SELF-SECURE
Outcome-obsessed	Skill-focused
Identity tied to external validation	Identity rooted in internal worth
High anxiety	Steady confidence
Reactive to criticism	Uses criticism constructively
Emotional volatility	Emotional steadiness

Here are the four tools we'll explore:

- **Focus on Skills, Not Outcomes.** Shift your attention to what you can control rather than what you cannot.
- **Take Nothing Personally.** Recognize others' reactions as reflections of their own experiences, not your worth.
- **What, Not How.** Learn to accept valuable feedback, regardless of its delivery.
- **Know Your Identity Beyond Performance.** Establish a stable self-worth, independent of external achievements.

Focus on Skills, Not Outcomes

"Focus on outcome = focusing on things you can't control and anxiety goes up. Instead, focus on your performance and the skills you can control = anxiety goes down and performance increases."
–Dr. Craig Manning

"Focus on the process, and the results will take care of themselves."
–Bill Walsh

What's one of the most anxiety-producing shots for an everyday golfer? Maybe it's the high-pressure putt for five bucks, or a tough tee shot over water. Those are tough. But for many, it's actually the #1 tee box where anxiety spikes highest. Why? The clubhouse is right there.

People might be watching. Suddenly, golfers worry more about not looking bad in front of the crowd than about their swing.

This focus on outcome creates anxiety, because it fixates on things outside their control:

- The outcome itself—
  Will the ball land on the fairway or in the rough?
- Others' opinions—
  How will the crowd, or social media, react if I fail?
- Self-worth tied to outcomes—
  Believing their worth hinges on this shot.

No wonder their anxiety shoots through the roof—and the dreaded "shankapottomus" emerges. Cue the classic excuses: "My back wasn't warmed up," or "I need a breakfast ball." The real issue, however, isn't physical—it's mental.

What if instead of worrying about outcomes, they focus solely on their skills—things completely within their control?

For example:

- Keeping their front arm straight during their backswing.
- Maintaining an easy, smooth swing tempo.
- Keeping their eyes fixed on the ball throughout contact.

Focusing on these skills reduces anxiety by placing attention firmly on factors within their control. As anxiety decreases, their chances of performing at their best increase significantly. Think of these skills as essential inputs—like dominoes lined up in sequence. Execute each skill consistently, and they maximize their likelihood of a successful outcome.

This isn't just about golf. Consider a basketball player facing critical free throws in the last seconds of a game. Most players in these high-pressure moments fixate on the outcome: "Will I make the shot or miss? What will people think if I choke?" Anxiety inevitably spikes, negatively affecting performance. Recently I watched Donovan Mitchell, one of my favorite basketball players, struggle at the free-throw line during a playoff game against the Pacers. He went 0 for 3 down the stretch, and his team lost. I bet he had outcome-focused thoughts running through his head.

If, instead, Mitchell had focused solely on controllable skills—like a good knee bend, eyes locked onto the back of the rim, and a confident, high follow-through—his anxiety would have dropped dramatically, likely improving his performance. I'm convinced that focusing on skills rather than outcomes would have made a difference. It certainly would have been for me during my biggest moment.

Heading into the Apple Cup, my mind wasn't centered on my skills—it was consumed by the approval I could gain from the game's outcome. I thought, "A win could make me the greatest Washington State quarterback ever," or "How will this game affect my NFL draft stock?" These thoughts came paired with fears: "What if I'm one of the few WSU quarterbacks who never wins an

Apple Cup? What will fans say? What will the media write? How will NFL coaches view me?"

With this pressure of *needing* approval tied to the outcome, guess what happened to my anxiety? It skyrocketed. I'd never experienced performance anxiety like this before. I never settled down, and when I finally did, it was far too late. Had I intentionally shifted my focus to my skills in the lead-up to that game, my performance and headspace undoubtedly would have been different.

So how exactly do you identify and cultivate these critical skills? Stick with me—I'll show you how. But first, it's important to understand what I've termed "The Paradox of Performance."

THE PARADOX OF PERFORMANCE

Here's how it works in its simplest form:

- Less Is More: The **less** you focus on outcomes and approval—the things you can't directly control—the **more** likely you are to achieve the results you desire.
- More Is Less: The **more** you obsess about outcomes and seek approval, the **less** likely you'll get the outcomes you truly want.

I shared this paradox over lunch with a high school buddy, who immediately related. In high school, basketball was his passion. He poured his energy, identity, and worth into it, relentlessly focusing on outcomes. The pressure weighed him down. Despite his effort, he felt he never reached his potential and fell short of the results he desperately wanted.

In contrast, tennis was a sport he played casually, almost as an afterthought. He didn't identify as a "tennis player," so he worried less about the results. Instead, he simply enjoyed playing, focusing solely on skills without anxiety over outcomes.

And guess what? By focusing less on results, he achieved more than he ever imagined—ending the year as a state champion.

Have you experienced something similar? This principle is powerful and universal:

- Less Is More: **Less** focus on outcome means **more** of the outcome you desire.
- More Is Less: **More** focus on outcome means **less** of the outcome you want.

CREATING AND CODING YOUR SKILLS

Skills are the foundation of strong mental performance. I teach my clients to categorize skills into three areas: physical, mental/emotional, and spiritual. Let's briefly unpack each one.

Physical Skills

Physical skills are tangible and technique-based—like the golfer maintaining a straight front arm, or a basketball player bending their knees at the free-throw line. Other examples include:

- Baseball: "Eyes on the seams."
- Running: "High knee drive."
- Swimming: "Head down, hips up."
- Soccer: "Strike through the ball."
- Football (QB): "Hitch in place."

Mental/Emotional Skills

Mental and emotional skills focus on internal thought processes and emotional regulation.

We began building our mental toolkit in Chapter 1 with skills such as:

- Take Ownership
- Control the Controllable
- Empowering Framing
- Gratitude Mindset

We'll continue adding to these throughout the book (some playbook techniques will blend them, such as 4-6 breathing, which is both physical and mental/emotional).

Spiritual Skills

Spiritual skills are what help you quiet the noise and play from a place of peace. They include powerful internal resets like *"clearing"*—a skill you'll learn in depth later—which allows you to release emotional clutter and reset your energy before competition. They also include practices like radical acceptance— letting go of what you can't control so you can lock in on what you can. These aren't soft skills. They're spiritual muscles. And just like any other skill in this playbook, it's not enough to know them. You've got to train them until they show up when the pressure hits. We'll explore these more deeply as we progress.

Now, simply knowing these skills isn't enough—you have to quickly recall and apply them under pressure. That's where "coding" comes in.

CODING YOUR SKILLS

Coding is about creating short, memorable phrases, typically just three to four words, that instantly trigger your understanding of a specific skill. Think of these coded phrases as a personal shorthand—a mental cue that helps you recall exactly what you need to do without being overwhelmed by too much information.

Why three to four words? Cognitive psychologist Alan Baddeley discovered that people can best remember three to four items briefly, about 20 seconds, before they're forgotten unless reinforced. Short, coded phrases make it easy to quickly retrieve your skills from memory exactly when you need them most.[6] Think of a computer—it holds a lot of information, but if it's not coded properly, you can't access it. The same goes for our skills.

For example, as a quarterback, I learned a skill from Tom House— the "throwing whisperer"—called *Eat the Burger*. This coded phrase meant that after throwing, my off-hand should be positioned as though holding an imaginary burger ready to take a bite. It instantly reminded me to keep all my throwing energy directed at the target rather than letting any leak away. Instead of a complex explanation, "Eat the Burger" immediately brought clarity and focus.

You see this concept everywhere in sports. The greatest coaching points and mantras are short and punchy:

- "Play the Next Play" (All Sports)
- "Run Through the Smoke" (Football Ball Carrier)
- "Ass to the Grass" (Fielder in Baseball)
- "Elbows at 90" (Running)
- "High and Tight" (Football Ball Carrier)

These phrases instantly communicate critical reminders without confusion, helping athletes execute efficiently under pressure.

Another great example of a coded skill that Kurt Warner reminded me of comes from the classic sports movie *For Love of the Game* starring Kevin Costner. Costner plays Billy Chapel, a legendary pitcher taking the mound at Yankee Stadium.

In one scene, the crowd is roaring, the subway rumbles in the distance, and fans are chanting. Then Chapel says his coded skill out loud: "*Clear the mechanism*." Instantly, all the noise fades. His focus sharpens. It's just him and his catcher.

It's a perfect illustration of a coded skill at work—a mental trigger that shifts your focus back to what matters most: what you can control. And if you're a sports fan, it's also an all-time great movie too.

HOW TO PUT YOUR SKILLS INTO ACTION

Once you've coded your skills, it's time to start using them. Before your next competition—whether it's practice, training, tryouts, or a game—write down three skills you want to focus on.

Then when you step into your competition, lock in on those skills.

Why? Because this shifts your focus away from things you can't control, like the outcome or other people's opinions, and places it on the things you can control. As a result, your anxiety decreases and your performance improves.

And here's the bonus: When you focus on executing your skills at a high level, your chances of getting the outcome you want go up. Skills are the inputs that lead to great results.

Remember the domino analogy? Execute on your skills, and you'll knock down the first domino, setting off the chain reaction that leads to high performance.

Pro Tip: Write your three skills on a sweatband and wear it during competition. Between plays, sets, or key moments, glance down to refocus. And if your mind starts to drift to things you can't control, use that glance as a reset—anchoring your focus back on the skills that matter most.

CODED SKILLS IN ACTION

Before our critical game against #19 UCLA in 2015, I wrote down three skills from my own Coded Skills Library:

1. "Can-Do Mindset."
2. "Be Decisive."
3. "Cool Hand Luke."

These were a shorthand for me to keep a "can-do" positive mindset throughout the game; to pull the trigger confidently, right or wrong; and to stay calm, cool, and collected.

They weren't easy to focus on. The game carried extra weight for me personally. A few years earlier, my family uprooted from Logan, Utah, to Southern California, chasing a football dream. My parents believed that our small town wasn't enough for me to get noticed. We left behind familiar comforts and landed at Oaks Christian High—home to celebrities' kids, BMWs, and luxury I'd never imagined. I felt completely out of place, alone, and overwhelmed. Family stress quickly followed. My parents separated temporarily, which contributed to my mom having a serious breakdown and to me not seeing either of my parents for an extended period of time. The entire experience unraveled quickly, ending with our return to Utah, feeling defeated, trying to pick up the pieces, and working to bring our family back together. Fast-forward four years—I was back in California at the Rose Bowl, now facing familiar Oaks Christian teammates across the field. The old anxieties returned. Could I prove I belonged here after all? Midway through the fourth quarter, with victory in sight, my mind momentarily drifted—back to outcomes, back to approval. That slip cost us. I threw an interception and UCLA took advantage, scoring quickly and turning the crowd's volume way up. At that moment, doubt surged. But Mind Strength isn't about perfection—it's about choosing how you respond. With just over a minute left, we trailed 27-24. I refocused:

- Can-Do Mindset: "We've still got this."
- Be Decisive: Trust my reads and throw confidently.
- Cool Hand Luke: Stay steady, no matter how intense the pressure.

On third and 10, with the game—and personal redemption—on the line, I took the snap, drifted right and threw decisively to Gabe Marks, who hauled it in for the game-winning touchdown with just three seconds left. I had my Hollywood ending, thanks entirely to refocusing on my coded skills and having a great team around me.

Now it's your turn.

Let's take these ideas and put them into action with your own personalized Mind Strength Playbook.

THE PLAYBOOK

BUILD YOUR CODED SKILLS LIBRARY

 Use the QR code to enter your *"Virtual Locker Room"* and access your "Coded Skills Library."

Step 1: Code Your Skills

Think of skills across all three categories—physical, mental/emotional, and spiritual—and simplify each one into a powerful, memorable three- to four-word phrase. Use phrases that resonate strongly with you.

Examples:

- Physical: "High Knee Drive" (Running), "Eyes on Target" (Football), "Easy Swing Tempo" (Golf).

- Mental/Emotional: "Control the Controllable," "Gratitude Mindset," "Empowering Framing."

- Spiritual: "Clear the Noise," "Total Acceptance," "Tune In," "Let It Go."

Step 2: Define Each Coded Skill Clearly

Next, write exactly what each code means to you. Here are a few examples of coded skills to help guide you:

- **Take Ownership**

No blaming circumstances or others. No entitlement. Look for and find solutions, not excuses.

- **Control the Controllable**

Direct your attention only toward what you can control. This focus lowers anxiety and boosts performance. Worrying about uncontrollable factors raises anxiety and reduces performance.

- **4-6 Breathing**

Calm your nerves by breathing in through your nose for 4 seconds, then out through your nose for 6 seconds.

- **Gratitude Mindset**

Intentionally focus on all the good you have rather than what you think you're lacking.

- **Empowering Framing**

Reframe challenges into positive opportunities. Instead of viewing setbacks negatively, tell yourself empowering stories: "This is making me stronger," or "It's setting up an epic comeback."

Step 3: Keep Adding to Your Library (Ongoing)

As we continue our Mind Strength journey, consistently update your Coded Skills Library. Each new chapter will introduce powerful skills you can add to your personal playbook, equipping you to handle any situation with confidence.

Final Note: Write Down and Focus on Three Skills Before Your Competition

Before you take the field or court, look at your Coded Skills Library and choose three skills to focus on for your competition. Write them down on a piece of paper, and if you want to take it a step further, write them on a sweatband or piece of tape that you wear. During the competition, keep anchoring back to those skills—not the outcome. The scoreboard will take care of itself when you consistently execute the things you can control.

Now you have a clear, concise way to remember and execute the skills that matter most—exactly when you need them.

 ## PARENT TIP

THE ALLURE AND RISKS OF TRANSFERRING

Be cautious about decisions to transfer schools, especially those involving a move or relocation. Consider carefully: Is your child driving this decision, or is it your ego stepping in? Remember, life is about more than sports. Make sure decisions are holistic and truly guided by your child's needs, with wise parental guidance.

In high school, I experienced two major transfers—one great, one disastrous. My freshman-year transfer to Logan was driven by me. My parents asked me openly, "If you could go to any school, where would it be?" Without hesitation, I chose Logan. I wanted a fresh start away from "daddy ball" and a football system ill-suited to my skillset. Logan offered family support, a spread offense, and a change I deeply desired. The result? A total success in every way—athletically, socially, emotionally. At Thanksgiving that year, I remember saying, "I'm so grateful we live in Logan."

But then we lost our way. My parents, influenced by a high-profile QB coach, made another move—to Southern California. This decision wasn't driven by me. It was fueled by dreams of higher status, greater success, and external validation. At my core, I didn't want it, and the resulting stress fractured our family and led to significant personal struggle.

Looking back, the difference is clear: Moves initiated by the child, driven by genuine holistic needs, tend to succeed. Decisions driven by parental ego, or society's scoreboard, often lead to regret.

Ask yourself honestly:

- Did my child initiate this move?

- Are they genuinely driving this decision?

- Will this benefit them holistically (beyond sports)?

- Is my ego influencing this decision more than their desires?

Choose wisely. Protect your family. Life is bigger than the scoreboard.

Take Nothing Personally

"Don't take anything personally. Nothing others do is because of you. What others say and do is a projection of their own reality, their own dream." –Don Miguel Ruiz (The Four Agreements)

Imagine interacting with two different people on the same day:

Person A went to bed early, woke refreshed, enjoyed a morning walk with their dog, and had their favorite breakfast: pancakes, bacon, eggs, syrup—the works. Arriving early to school, they felt relaxed and prepared for their test.

Person B, however, stayed up late cramming and fell asleep at their desk, waking stiff and panicked after oversleeping. Their dog took forever on their morning walk, finally choosing the neighbor's pristine lawn—complete with a "Kindly keep your pets off our lawn" sign.

Midway through the dog's business, the neighbor appeared angrily, and worse yet, Person B had forgotten a dog bag. Embarrassed and stressed, they rushed to school without breakfast, sliding into class sweaty, breathless, and just in time for a test they realized they'd studied the wrong material for.

Who do you think would treat you more kindly, patiently, and understandingly that day? Clearly, Person A.

Notice, I didn't mention your behavior or your words toward either of them. Yet, instinctively, you knew how they'd each respond had nothing to do with you—it depended entirely on what they were experiencing internally.

This scenario isn't rare; it's everyday life. I learned from Don Miguel Ruiz in *The Four Agreements* that what others say or do isn't about you at all. It reflects their inner reality, emotions, struggles, and perceptions—not your worth or value.

Think about that carefully: If what people say or do is truly about their own internal experiences, why would we ever tie our self-worth or happiness to their approval?

We shouldn't—and don't have to. Needing approval based on others' reactions is a losing formula. Remember, their actions reflect them—not you. *Take nothing personally.*

THE METAPHORICAL MIRROR

Imagine you and I are standing face-to-face. You're holding a mirror, and I have a laser pointer aimed directly at you. But because of the mirror you're holding, where does the laser end up? Back on me.

This visual illustrates the Mind Strength skill of "Take Nothing Personally." When someone directs negativity toward you, remember it's not about you—it's a reflection of them, their internal state, their struggles. Your job is simple: Hold up your mirror and reflect it back, staying off the emotional "teeter-totter" of needing approval.

Too often, though, we drop our mirror. We absorb the negativity, criticism, or harsh words, allowing ourselves to ride the highs and lows dictated by others' opinions. Keep your mirror up. This gives you a stable, secure foundation, free from the emotional ups and downs.

👟 WALK-ON WISDOM

HOLDING UP YOUR MIRROR WITH FANS AND THE MEDIA

*"Cali Reject!" *Hands clapping.* "Cali Reject!" *Hands clapping.**

I had just fouled out in a high school rivalry basketball game. As I walked off the court, the opposing student section—and even some parents—piled on, mocking me and reminding me of my failed move to California.

That was my first real taste of the highs and lows of being in the public eye. Later in my career, I heard it all:

"Falk, we love you!"

"Falk is King of the North!" (*Game of Thrones* fans)

"Falk for president!"

And the next:

"Bench Falk!"

"F*** you, Falk—you suck!"

The media was no different. One article praised me. Another called for my job. If you play the game long enough—sports, business, or any arena where you put yourself out there—fans, critics, and outside noise all come with the territory. (I'm sure the same process will happen with this book.)

These moments are when the metaphorical mirror becomes essential. Let praise pass through you without clinging to it. Let criticism pass without it sticking. Hold up the mirror, reflect everything back, while you stay rooted in your identity, your preparation, and your mission. Stay off the "Teeter-Totter Trap."

I once saw Tom Brady reference a quote that has stuck with me ever since. It's given me perspective in these moments and shaped how I handle both the cheers and the jeers. It's from Theodore Roosevelt, and I believe every athlete, leader, and public performer should know it and internalize it:

"It is not the critic who counts;

not the man who points out how the strong man stumbles,
or where the doer of deeds could have done them better.

The credit belongs to the man who is actually in the arena,
whose face is marred by dust and sweat and blood;

who strives valiantly; who errs, who comes short again and again,
because there is no effort without error and shortcoming;

but who does actually strive to do the deeds;

who knows great enthusiasms, the great devotions;

who spends himself in a worthy cause;

who at the best knows in the end the triumph of high achievement,

and who at the worst, if he fails,

at least fails while daring greatly,

so that his place shall never be with those cold

and timid souls who neither know victory nor defeat."

Hold up your mirror. Reflect the noise. Play with everything you've got. Because you?

You're the lucky one in the arena.

 THE PLAYBOOK

REFRAMING THE MIRROR

Pull out your Mind Strength Playbook and complete the following exercise to practice the "Take Nothing Personally" skill:

Step 1: Reflect

- Recall a recent interaction where someone's criticism or negativity upset you.

- Write down what was said and briefly describe how you chose to feel.

Step 2: Hold Up Your Mirror

- Imagine holding up your metaphorical mirror, reflecting their negativity back to them.

- Ask yourself: "What might this person's harsh words or negativity really be about? What personal struggles or emotions might be influencing them?"

Step 3: Reframe

- Write down a new interpretation of this interaction, now recognizing it wasn't personal but a reflection of the other person's inner state.

  For example:

  - Original: "They criticized me because I'm not good enough."

  - Reframed: "Their criticism likely came from their own stress, insecurity, or frustration, not from my worth."

Step 4: Code and Anchor the Skill

- Choose a brief coded phrase (e.g., "Take Nothing Personally," "Not About Me," "Reflect It," "Hold My Mirror") to quickly trigger this mindset in future interactions.

Continue adding examples to your playbook whenever you feel emotionally triggered by others, reinforcing this powerful skill over time.

MODELING "TAKE NOTHING PERSONALLY"

Your kids learn more by watching you than from what you tell them. Demonstrate emotional maturity by practicing "Take Nothing Personally" openly and clearly in front of them.

Next time you're criticized or frustrated by someone else's words or actions:

- Verbally reflect in front of your child: "You know what? That person's having a tough day. Their reaction wasn't really about me."

- Show them how you hold up your metaphorical mirror and keep calm rather than getting caught in emotional highs and lows.

- By modeling emotional steadiness, you're equipping your child with a critical life skill: the ability to remain grounded, confident, and emotionally resilient in any situation.

What, Not How

Learning to not take things personally can be tough. Especially if the feedback comes from a coach or mentor. Thus why the "What, Not How" skill is so critical. And something I've definitely had to learn.

"Falk, you've got to be the slowest mother… *cough* …mother f'er I've ever seen!" Coach Leach snapped, his voice catching on his signature rasp. "I'm… *cough* … so damn tired of watching you stand there like an f'ing statue taking sack after sack."

Coach Leach continued this tirade for ten brutal minutes following our humiliating 37-3 loss to Cal Berkeley, statistically my worst collegiate game ever. Five interceptions, including an impossibly bad shovel-pass pick. It wasn't my night.

Earlier in my career, a delivery like this—especially in front of teammates—would have crushed me. I would have mentally checked out for the season, crippled by embarrassment and anxiety. But by this point, I'd learned a critical skill: I needed to shift my mindset from how feedback was delivered to what was being said.

Players often crave their coaches' approval, so harsh criticism can feel devastating. Early in college, desperate for Coach Leach's approval, I felt euphoric when praised and hopeless when criticized. This emotional teeter-totter affected my performance on the field and happiness off of it. It wasn't sustainable.

I needed a better way. Inspired by Tom Brady—who credits the book *The Four Agreements* as foundational—I studied how to detach my worth from criticism. Brady's approach was clear: Avoid personalizing feedback; simply identify what you can learn. Observing my coaches closely, I realized their delivery matched their mood—it wasn't about me.

During a long, reflective walk around campus, it clicked: "What, Not How."

- **What** is the useful coaching point here?
- **Not How** is it being delivered to me?

When Coach Leach blasted me about taking sacks, I focused on the what: "Get rid of the ball quicker. No negative plays." He was right—I took nine sacks that game, none of which were the line's fault. Accepting this truth helped me own it and grow, rather than spiral into self-doubt and pity because of how it was said.

This mental shift was transformational. It stabilized my emotions and turned tough feedback into actionable advice. Instead of interference, Coach Leach became an asset, helping me become a better player.

THE PLAYBOOK

"WHAT," NOT "HOW"

Use your Mind Strength Playbook to practice this powerful skill:

Step 1: Identify a recent criticism.

Write down something critical someone said to you—perhaps a coach, parent, teacher, or friend. Be specific about what was said and how you felt initially.

Step 2: Separate *What* from *How.*

- Clearly identify the **"What"**: What's the valuable insight or feedback hidden within this criticism?
- Note the **"How"**: How did their delivery or tone affect your reaction?

Step 3: Reframe positively.

- Rewrite the criticism, removing emotion and focusing strictly on the useful information or skill you can apply.

  Example:

    - Original: "You're playing lazy defense!" (harsh tone)
    - Extracted What: "I need to move my feet faster and be more active defensively."

Step 4: Code and Anchor the Skill

- Create a short phrase to quickly recall this mindset during criticism (e.g., "Find the Gold" "What, Not How").

COACHING TIP

BE MINDFUL OF DELIVERY

Coaches, remember: Your athletes naturally seek your approval, making your words incredibly impactful. Be intentional about your delivery. Your job is to elevate performance and confidence, not trigger their walls and defenses to go up.

Regularly ask yourself:

- Am I providing constructive, actionable feedback, or am I venting my own frustrations?
- Do I know the communication style each athlete responds best to?

Your mindfulness directly influences your players' growth, performance, and emotional well-being. Use your influence wisely.

Know Your Identity Beyond Performance

"Either way, you are putting yourself on a slippery slope when you start believing that the outcome of your effort represents or embodies who you really are as a person—what your value as a person is." –Bill Walsh

When athletes retire, whether by choice or not, many experience something they never expected: identity loss. The same thing happens to those who reach the top of the mountain. You achieve what you always dreamed of... and then feel empty. *Is this it?* you wonder.

Why? Because your identity has been built on performance. On how others see you. On approval. On society's scoreboard—likes, rankings, contracts, applause.

I've been there.

At the peak of my college career, I was the guy. *SportsCenter.* Scott Van Pelt. Packed stadiums. Getting 450 text messages after a USC win. Free meals. Everyone wanted something from me.

And then?

I got cut by the New York Jets after a rough outing against the Eagles. Ten people reached out. Minshew Mania was in full bloom, and I was quickly forgotten.

That's when the teeter-totter dropped—and hard. I wasn't just dealing with rejection from the league. I was dealing with something deeper. Something that forced me to ask: *If I'm not the quarterback anymore, who am I?*

This started my "quarter-life crisis." Not just rediscovering who I was—but learning for the first time.

Because the truth I'd ignored for so long finally surfaced:

Your sport is what you do—not who you are.

That doesn't just apply to athletes. I know my dad went through the same identity crisis after he sold his company and he was no longer the CEO. He battled the same question: *Who am I?*

Whatever your title is—athlete, coach, performer, CEO, musician—it's not your identity.

Who you are is deeper than any scoreboard, highlight reel, or P&L.

Your worth is not earned—it's given. Inherent. God-given. And no outcome can ever change it.

That truth is easy to say but hard to live. And I'll admit I've wrestled with it deeply. I still do. But I'm getting better. And when I remember who I really am—not for what I achieve, but for who I was created to be—the anxiety fades. The pressure lifts. And peace sets in.

Here's a poem I wrote during one of those low moments—one I think someone reading this might need to hear:

"Who cares what they think? I surely do.
Every move I've made I thought of the review.
How will I look? And what will they say?
Will I win their love and approval for one more day?
Why do I do this? How can it be?
Does it all stem from a deep root of a lack of love for me?
And if this is so... How then do I grow?
The answer becomes clear...
Start loving the man who is standing in the mirror."

That's your invitation: To love who you are. To stop chasing worth.

To choose a new scoreboard—one rooted in truth, not approval.

⚡ THE PLAYBOOK

IDENTITY BEYOND PERFORMANCE

Use your Mind Strength Playbook to root your identity in truth, not achievement.

Step 1: Inventory Your Labels

Write down the roles or titles you've associated with your identity (e.g., "Athlete," "Straight-A Student," "Captain," "Performer"). Be honest about how much of your self-worth is tied to them.

Step 2: Ask the Deeper Question

For each label, ask: If I lost this tomorrow, would I still know who I am?

Step 3: Recenter in Truth

Now write three to five identity truths that are not performance-based. These might include:

- "I am loved."
- "I am strong in my values."
- "I matter because of who I am—not what I do."
- "My worth is unchanging."
- "I am part of something greater" (Adapt or revise based on personal beliefs.)

Step 4: Code It

Create a coded identity skill—just like we've done before. Short. Sticky. Anchoring.

Examples:

- "Bigger Than Ball"
- "Play With Perspective"
- "Anchor, Not Outcome"
- "Worthy, Win or Lose"

When the pressure comes, say your identity skill out loud. Remind yourself of what's true. Anchor in that—not the scoreboard.

PARENT TIP

AVOID VICARIOUSLY LIVING THROUGH YOUR KID

"The greatest burden a child must bear is the unlived life of the parent."—Carl Jung

Growing up, I saw and experienced this firsthand.

From a young age, my sisters were singer-songwriters, traveling across the country (and sometimes the world) trying to "make it." My mom was the one steering the ship. She became their momager—booking gigs, managing logistics, and doing everything in her power to push their careers forward.

When it came to my sports, she brought that same intensity. She would do whatever it took for us to be successful. Because at her core, my mom was living vicariously through us. Our wins were her wins. Our losses were her losses.

That mindset followed me to Washington State. As I started to experience success, she gladly embellished the role of "the quarterback's mom." Her sense of worth became tied to how I performed. She would boast it, post it, and proudly vocalize her son's success to any and all who were willing to hear—because after all, it was her success. It was all about optics. About how people saw us as a family. About how they saw her.

Then our careers shifted.

She wasn't the momager or "the quarterback's mom" anymore. Without those roles, she didn't know who she was. Her identity had been so deeply entangled with ours that when our professional paths changed, she was left feeling lost and unraveled. That loss didn't just affect her—it sent ripples through our whole family.

Here's the thing—it's natural to be emotionally connected to your children. It's normal to ride the highs and lows. But this took it to another level. When you feel like your parent's emotional state depends entirely on your performance, when their identity is riding on how well you do, the pressure *to lift them up* becomes suffocating. You, the child, become their lifeblood. You know that their identity and emotional state is riding on you and the outcome you produce. You then carry the *weight*. The *burden*. Quietly. Constantly.

How to replace this?

I once heard a relationship analogy that's stuck with me—and I think it applies perfectly here:

Be like **two eggs, sunny-side up**.

The whites can overlap and be all over each other—love each other, support each other, be close.

But the yolks? They stay separate.

Your identity should remain distinct from your kids.

Because when your self-worth comes from within, not from how your kids perform, you unlock their chains and create a healthier foundation for them to grow… and for you to remain whole, even when their journey takes a different path.

Chapter 2 Review— Overcome an Athlete's Biggest Hurdle: *Needing* Approval

This chapter unpacked one of the most dangerous traps an athlete—or any person—can fall into: tying their identity and performance to external approval. We explored four powerful mindset shifts that help build true inner strength and allow you to become more self-secure.

- **Focus on Skills, Not Outcomes:** Outcomes are uncontrollable. Skills are not. Performance improves when you focus on inputs, not results.
- **Take Nothing Personally:** What others say and do is about them, not you. Use your metaphorical mirror and stay grounded in self-worth.
- **"What," Not "How":** Detach from tone. Focus on truth. Even harsh feedback can become fuel if you know how to receive it.
- **Know Your Identity Beyond Performance:** You are not your stat line. You are not your title. Your value doesn't swing with public opinion—it's already set.

If you remember nothing else, remember this:

You are worthy. You are loved. You don't need to earn it.

When you stop needing approval, your mind quiets. Your anxiety fades. Your performance rises. Because now, it's coming from the inside.

CHAPTER 3

Reset Your Internal Success Thermostat

*"Each of us has an inner thermostat setting
that determines how much love, success, and creativity
we allow ourselves to enjoy.*

*When we exceed our inner thermostat setting,
we will often do something to sabotage ourselves,
causing us to drop back into the old, familiar zone
where we feel secure."*

–Gay Hendricks (The Big Leap)

The Game That Turned Cold

Friday the 13th. Berkeley, California.

We were on a roll, a perfect season.

We were undefeated—6-0. Ranked eighth in the country. We'd just taken down #5 USC at home and beat Oregon on the road. The season was shaping up to be historic. I was in the Heisman conversation. The NFL was in sight.

And it all changed in the blink of an eye and five interceptions later. Our perfect record? Gone. My Heisman hopes? Crushed.

It was the worst statistical performance of my career. And looking back, I understand exactly what happened. I didn't just have a bad game, I had a subconscious reset. I'd outperformed the identity I believed about myself, and my mind did what it was wired to do: It brought me back to familiar territory. I had surpassed my internal success thermostat.

Let me explain.

Imagine a thermostat set to 72 degrees. If the room drops to 68, the heat kicks on to bring it back up. If the room climbs to 78, the air conditioning turns on to bring it back down.

Thermostats regulate the temperature and return a space to its set point.

This is what happens in our lives. We have an internal thermostat—a subconscious setting for how much success we feel comfortable with.

When we dip below our inner success temperature—when things aren't going well—we grind. We lock in. Our "heat" kicks in and we fight to get back to that familiar level.

Unfortunately, the opposite is true as well. When we start to exceed our internal thermostat—when we find ourselves in a new territory, performing better than we're used to—something inside us panics. And instead of rising with the moment, we sabotage it. We do things unconsciously or consciously to pull ourselves back to a level of success that feels familiar and comfortable.

That's what I did that night.

At Washington State, I was the walk-on. I was used to being the underdog. It was a part of my identity. But leading the eighth-ranked team in the country, in the Heisman conversation and almost a shoo-in to get drafted in the NFL... that was way beyond my comfort level.

So what did I do? I unraveled it. I played the worst game of my career and brought myself back down to the level of success I felt comfortable with. And I wasn't alone. Our entire team had built our identity around being scrappy and underrated. We were the no-stars team who prided ourselves on grit. That night, at the top of the Pac-12 with the opportunity to keep rising to higher heights, our collective thermostat flipped the AC on. We stopped rising.

We stopped believing we belonged. And we brought ourselves back down to the team we were comfortable being.

But it started with me.

How do we stop that cycle? How do we train ourselves to develop the Mind Strength to raise our internal success thermostat instead of resetting it every time we level up? You don't start with talent—you start with belief.

Recognize It Starts With Belief

"Our only limitations are those we set up in our own minds"
–Napoleon Hill

In high school, I used to think confidence was something you were born with. You either believed in yourself or you didn't. You either had that inner edge or you didn't. I thought that whatever belief systems you had, that was what you were going to be stuck with. There was nothing you could do to change it.

But my perspective shifted when I read Wayne Dyer's work. Through his work, I discovered that you absolutely can change a belief system.

It's not easy, but it's possible.

Changing a belief system is similar to that of changing your physical body. You don't walk into a weight room, do a hundred crunches, and walk out with a six-pack. You don't go for one run and expect to be in shape. And yet, in strengthening the mind, that's exactly the unrealistic expectation athletes have. They work on some Mind Strength principles for a few days in a row or maybe a week, and suddenly expect to have it all come together for them.

This isn't realistic. Just as you need daily work and training for your body, you also need it for your mind. If you want a healthy body, you build it—rep by rep, day by day.

Eat clean.

Train smart. Sleep right.

Do it long enough, and the results show up.

Your belief system works the same way.

If you feed your mind strong, clear thoughts…

If you stay consistent…

If you let go of what's no longer serving you…

Then, over time, your mental muscles grow. Your internal thermostat rises. You start to operate at a new level because you trained for it.

WHAT IS A BELIEF SYSTEM?

I use Dr. Craig Manning's definition to define belief systems: "A belief system is an attitude that something is true."

That's it.

It's not magic. It's not personality. It's just an inner stance.

If you believe in a certain religion, you have an attitude that the doctrine is true.

If you believe you're a clutch performer, you have the attitude of a clutch performer.

If you believe you're not athletic enough, you have an attitude that reflects that and leaks into everything—how you train, how you show up, how you recover from mistakes.

How does a belief system get created?

Wayne Dyer taught that belief systems are built on "thoughts repeated over a long period of time."

The same way muscles are built through repetition, a belief system is created through repeating thoughts. Over and over, you think the same thing, and that thought becomes your belief.

"I always choke in big games."

"I'm not fast enough to play at the next level."

"No one believes in me, so why should I?"

Say it enough, and you won't just think it, you'll start living it. Not because it's true, but because your mind has accepted that belief system as true.

CAN A BELIEF SYSTEM BE CHANGED?

Yes. Absolutely.

Because if thoughts built your belief system, then new thoughts can rebuild it.

You don't need a personality transplant. You need a training plan. And that starts with knowing what kind of thoughts to focus on.

According to Dr. Wayne Dyer, we have two types of thoughts:

- Strengthening Thoughts—build belief, boost confidence, increase clarity.
- Weakening Thoughts—drain belief, create fear, lower your thermostat.

Some coaches and psychologists add a third category: Neutral Thoughts—thoughts that don't strengthen or weaken you, like "What am I eating for dinner?" But for Mind Strength purposes, we're not interested in those. We're after attaining more strengthening thoughts and releasing the weakening ones.

Because here's the chain:

Strengthening thoughts → Strong belief system → Elevated thermostat → Higher performance.

It works. And it's trainable.

The problem is, most athletes don't even know what they're repeating. They just run the same inner script they picked up years ago. Maybe from a coach. Maybe from a parent. Maybe from one bad game in ninth grade.

They don't know they can question it, rewire it, and raise it. But you can, so let's get to work.

OUT WITH THE OLD, IN WITH THE NEW

Over the years, I developed a tool to help me take control—to intentionally choose the belief systems I wanted and remove the thoughts that were holding me back. I know it can help you do the same.

It's five easy steps:

1. **Identify Your Inner Critic.** Name the thoughts that are holding you back.
2. **Trace Their Origin.** Find out where those thoughts started and why they stuck.
3. **Turn the Lights On.** Disempower the belief by flipping on the light and exposing the weak beliefs for what they are.
4. *Clear* **Your Inner Critic.** Forgive, release, and free your energy to perform.
5. **Create New Thoughts.** Create "I *am*" statements that elevate your identity.

Let's dive in.

1. Identify Your Inner Critic

"A higher concept of yourself involves taking on new truths and shedding your old views of what you can achieve." –Wayne Dyer

Before you can rewrite the story, you have to know what story you're telling yourself.

That starts with identifying your Inner Critic—the voice inside your head that doesn't just doubt you, it defines you in the wrong way.

In my coaching sessions, I hear these all the time:

- *"I'm not good enough."*
- *"I'm not smart enough."*
- *"I'm not athletic enough."*
- *"I'm not a leader."*
- *"I'll never make it."*

These aren't just thoughts—they're belief seeds. Left unchecked, they become identity.

I had mine too. These were the three thoughts that followed me everywhere heading into college:

- *"Not athletic enough to play quarterback."*
- *"Don't have a strong enough arm."*
- *"Can't perform in the clutch."*

I carried these thoughts with me, and the more I repeated them— even silently—the more true they became in my mind. That's how the thermostat gets set too low. That's how potential gets capped.

So let's find out what you've been carrying.

⅀ THE PLAYBOOK

IDENTIFY YOUR OWN INNER CRITIC

Write down three Inner Critic thoughts that show up for you most often. Be honest. Be real. No filter.

If you're stuck, ask:

- What do I say to myself after I make a mistake?

- What doubts show up before big moments?

- What voice do I hear when things get quiet?

If you don't have three? No problem. Write what you've got. And if you're the rare unicorn who doesn't hear an Inner Critic right now, read on anyway. You'll want these tools when that voice does show up.

Once you've written them down, pause. Take a breath. These thoughts aren't you—but they've been in you. This is the first step in changing that.

Next, we'll figure out where they came from.

2. Trace Their Origin

"Until you make the unconscious conscious, it will rule your life and people will call it fate." –Carl Jung

Once you've identified your Inner Critic, it's time to ask a deeper question: Where did this voice come from?

Because here's the truth: Unless you bring those origins into the light, they'll keep running the show from the shadows.

This step is about taking the driver's seat back.

A good tool in helping identify where these come from is to ask yourself some questions:

- Is there a person you think of when you think of this "Inner Critic" thought/belief?
- Is there a time you compared yourself to somebody else?
- Is there a past moment or game that comes to mind?

Let me walk you through how I've traced my own.

"Not athletic enough to play quarterback."

I think of being in Youth Football. I was playing tight end—a glorified offensive lineman at that age—and my coach used to call out across the field, "Falk, you're last again," on top of other comments and actions. They stuck. I chose then to have the thought "Not athletic enough to play quarterback"

"Don't have a strong enough arm."

I think of competing at an Elite 11 camp going into my sophomore year of high school. During warm-ups, they paired us up and drilled our arm strength by having us get down on both knees and throw the ball back and forth to each other. As we continued to move further and further back, my football started one-hopping to get to my partner, while he could have drilled a hole through my chest as he fired laser after laser toward me. I chose to have the thought "I don't have a strong enough arm."

"Can't perform in the clutch."

I think of two past games. It's my freshman year in high school and our team's got a perfect season going. We just scored with a few seconds remaining in the game and are now down by one point. We elect to go for two and win it all. But instead of throwing a game-winning pass, I throw the ball at my wide receiver's feet and all of my efforts come up short.

Senior season, rivalry game, the ball is in my hands at the end for an opportunity to win it with great field position… Turnover on downs. Game over.

After these games, I chose to have the thought, "I can't perform in the clutch."

 ## THE PLAYBOOK

TRACE YOUR INNER CRITIC'S ORIGIN

Go back to the list you made in step 1. For each Inner Critic thought, ask yourself:

- Is there a specific person you associate this belief with? Who said it? Who implied it? Who modeled it?

- Did it come from comparison? A teammate, rival, sibling, influencer—someone who seemed better, faster, stronger?

- Was there a moment or game that planted it? A mistake, a loss, a moment where things didn't go your way?

Use these prompts to help you trace the origin of each belief.

Then, next to each Inner Critic thought on your list, jot down what you discover:

- "Not athletic enough to play quarterback." $\longrightarrow$ Youth Football coach.

- "Can't perform in the clutch." $\longrightarrow$ Freshman two-point play, senior rivalry loss.

This step matters because you can't change what you won't confront.

Once you see where a belief started, you stop treating it like fate—and start treating it like a decision.

3. Turn the Lights On

Your Inner Critic only has power in the dark. Flip on the light, and you'll see it's not truth—just falsehoods you've dressed up like authority.

What happens when you turn on the lights in a dark room?

The darkness disappears.

That's exactly what we're doing in this step.

You've named your Inner Critic thoughts.

You've traced them back to where they started.

Now it's time to turn on the lights and expose the weakening thoughts and beliefs that have been holding you back.

Because these beliefs—they aren't you. They're just stories you've falsely created, and once you see them clearly, you can begin to shed those old beliefs and replace them with ones that actually serve you.

When you shine the light of awareness on them—when you see them clearly, without shame or fear—you take away their power. You stop letting them define you, and you start deciding who you want to be.

In my experience, these Inner Critic thoughts usually stem from four major sources:

- **Empty Wells**—people who weren't qualified to define you but whose words stuck anyway.
- **Comparison**—looking sideways at others and using their performance to judge your worth.
- **Previous "Bad" or "Failed" Performances**—a moment (or several) when you fell short and started believing that was your identity.

- **"Haven't Done It Before"**—doubting yourself just because you've never done something before.

Each of these sources can create deep roots in your belief system. But each one can be challenged, cleared, and replaced.

EMPTY WELLS

Imagine you're lost in the desert and you've spent all day walking underneath an unforgiving sun without a single drop of water to quench your thirst. Finally, you come upon a well, but when you go to drink, it's empty.

It doesn't matter how thirsty you are. The well isn't going to hydrate you. It's empty. No matter how hard you might try, you cannot drink from an empty well.

Yet, in our lives, we drink from "empty wells" all the time. We allow people who aren't qualified to give us opinions on certain issues or topics and dictate how we feel about ourselves, blind to the fact that there is no actual substance behind their opinions.

We all have "empty wells" in our story. I drank from one in Youth Football when I let my coach influence my belief system and told myself that I was "not athletic enough to play quarterback."

As I got older and started doing the work, I finally stopped and asked: Was that coach even a credible source, or was he just an empty well? Let's break it down:

- What was the highest level of football he played?
  High school.
- What was the highest level he coached?
  Youth Football.
- Any conflict of interest?
  His son—same age—played quarterback.

That's not a well. That's a dry hole in the ground.

He wasn't like my high school coach, who's now in the Utah High School Football Hall of Fame and developed multiple Division I quarterbacks. That guy had a resume. This one? He had a whistle and a bias.

So why was I letting his words shape my belief system?

Through this process, I can see that I created a disempowering story for myself by drinking from an "empty well." And just as I made the decision to allow this Inner Critic thought to become part of my identity, I can now start the process of disempowering it and turning the lights on to see it for what it really is.

THE PLAYBOOK

EXPOSE THE EMPTY WELLS

Go back to your Inner Critic list and look at the origin stories you wrote. Now ask yourself honestly: Did any of those thoughts come from someone who wasn't qualified to define you?

A coach who lacked experience.

A teammate who was insecure.

A parent who meant well but didn't know the whole picture.

A teacher, scout, sibling, or random voice online.

If so, label it. Write "(Empty Well)" next to that origin. This is your way of saying: "This belief came from someone I no longer give authority to."

Here's what that might look like in your notes:

- "Not athletic enough to play quarterback."—Youth Football coach (Empty Well)

- "Not smart enough for college ball."—Eighth-grade teacher (Empty Well)

By calling it what it is, you take the sting out and remove the false authority.

You make the unconscious conscious—which, as Carl Jung said, is the only way to stop it from ruling your life.

This is your chance to take ownership and draw a line in the sand. To say: "This may have shaped me, but it no longer defines me."

COMPARISON
"Comparison is the thief of joy." –Theodore Roosevelt

Comparison is a confidence killer.

In my life, my coaching sessions, and my own playing career, I've seen this trap take down more athletes than anything else. It sneaks in quietly—usually when we're scrolling, scouting, or sizing ourselves up next to someone else—and suddenly, the Inner Critic has fuel.

When you compare yourself to others, one of two things happens—and neither of them builds your Mind Strength or increases your performance:

- **You perceive other people to be further ahead of you.** This knocks your confidence and plants the seeds for these Inner Critic thoughts and beliefs. You start thinking you're behind, not enough, already losing, and that self-doubt spreads fast.

- **You perceive yourself to be further ahead of other people.** You might feel a quick hit of confidence—but it's built on sand. The moment they pass you, the tide comes in and washes your confidence away. Or you don't push yourself as hard as you should because you are "already better than them." This type of mentality stifles growth.

Comparison throws you right back onto that Teeter-Totter Trap and its anxiety-producing impacts.

When you're "up," life is good. You feel secure. When you're "down," life feels like it's falling apart. But either way, your focus is on them—not you.

And here's the real danger:

Comparison shifts your attention to the external. When you fixate on other people and things outside of your control, your anxiety rises and your performance decreases.

To escape this trap, you have to recenter your focus on something you can control: progress.

I fell into this trap my sophomore year. I went to the Elite 11 camp at TCU. It's one of the top quarterback competitions in the country. Most guys there were juniors and seniors. I was only a sophomore with barely any camp experience, competing against players who had trained extensively for a number of years.

As I compared myself to my warm-up partner, I thought, "I don't have a strong enough arm." And that became my belief.

It didn't matter that I'd added 7 yards to my throw since my freshman year. All I saw was the gap between him and me—and I let that gap define me.

But years later, as I did this work, I saw the situation clearly:

- He was older.
- He was more experienced.
- I was progressing faster than I realized.

The real mistake wasn't my arm strength. It was focusing on him instead of my own growth. I missed the opportunity to gain confidence from my progress because I was too busy focusing on comparing myself with everyone else.

That *aha* moment—years later, as I was heading into college—was another major turning point. It helped me flip on the light, see the situation for what it really was, take ownership, and begin unlocking the Inner Critic chains tied to that belief. From there, I could finally shift my focus back to what mattered: my own progress and growth.

👟 WALK-ON WISDOM

POSITION BATTLES—COCOON YOURSELF

I've been part of more position battles than I can count—both as a player and now as a coach helping athletes navigate that same pressure-filled terrain.

In football, most coaches will tell you, "Watch the other quarterback. Take notes. Study the defense. Get mental reps." I did that. And you know what it got me? Stuck on the teeter-totter of comparison.

When the other QB made a great play, I felt like I had to one-up him. Hero ball. When he struggled, I felt relief heading into my rep. Either way, I was riding a rollercoaster that I couldn't control, and my performance suffered.

So I made a shift. I did something counterintuitive to what the coaches were preaching. I didn't watch his reps at all. I "cocooned" myself.

While he was up, I was warming up. I was mentally reviewing my **three coded skills**, reciting affirmations, and prepping for my moment. I detached from *his* reps and reattached to *mine*.

Same thing in the film room. I didn't watch his clips. I drew up my plays from the script and watched only when I was up. If Coach Leach made a coaching point, I listened. If he repeated it, I'd glance at the film. But that was it.

The coaches also used to print out practice stats and leave them on our desk. Before this shift, I'd frantically scan to see where I ranked. Afterward? I'd close my eyes, push the sheet to the center of the table, and lock back in on my process.

Even outside the facility, if someone brought up the QB battle or sent me articles, I'd shut it down. "I'm focused internally. I don't need that noise." I became like a racehorse with blinders on—focused only on my lane.

The result?

Way less anxiety. Way more control. Way better performance.

My clients? Same results.

If you're in a position battle right now—**"cocoon" yourself**.

Detach from the distractions. Anchor into your process and progress. Control the controllables.

And let the rest take care of itself.

THE PLAYBOOK

SHIFT THE LENS

Go back to your list of Inner Critic origins. Now ask yourself:

- Did I fall into comparison? Was I judging myself against someone older, stronger, or more experienced? Was I basing my worth on where I stacked up—not how far I'd come?

If so, write "(Comparison)" next to that belief.

Then underneath it, jot down at least one area of personal progress you missed at the time.

Example:

- "Don't have a strong enough arm."—Elite 11 (Comparison)

→ But I had added 7 yards to my deep ball since my freshman year.

This is how you shift the lens from external scoreboard → to internal scoreboard. From self-doubt → to measurable progress.

You can't always control where you are on the path. But you can control the steps you take today. That's Mind Strength.

PAST "BAD" OR "FAILED" PERFORMANCES

This might be the most common "Inner Critic" seed there is. Athletes use a previous performance or experience that didn't go their way as "evidence" to prove that their negative beliefs about themselves are true.

This was the root of my third Inner Critic thought, "Can't perform in the clutch," that I shared earlier. I used my poor performance in those two high school games as evidence that I wasn't a clutch player. And that belief followed me for years until I turned on the lights and shifted my story.

Here's what I've learned: Past outcomes aren't permanent. They don't define you unless you let them. A failed performance in the past doesn't dictate your future performances as long as you learn from your mistakes and apply the knowledge.

Take my daughter, for example.

When she was learning to walk, she stumbled and fell. A lot. And if she had the mindset of most athletes, she would have thought, "I must not be a good walker. I won't ever be able to walk." But that's not how growth works. Instead, she fell, learned, adjusted, and tried again. And eventually? She walked. Then she ran. And now we can't keep up with her.

It's the same thing as riding a bike. You didn't fall off once and decide, "I guess I'll just never be able to ride a bike." No, you got back on, you learned, and you improved. So why don't we give ourselves that same grace when it comes to performance? Why do we allow ourselves to have a fixed mindset?

Here's a formula to change your mindset and start watering seeds of growth instead of your Inner Critic seeds.

1. An outcome is produced.

2. Learn from the outcome.

3. Apply the learning the next time.

That's it.

It breaks the cycle of shame and replaces it with ownership and growth. Here's how this formula played out in my own life:

- An outcome is produced: I wasn't clutch in two key high school games.
- Learn from the outcome: I let my nerves take over. I focused on what others would think—coaches, recruiters, fans—instead of locking in on my skills and what I could control.
- Apply the learning the next time: In future clutch moments, I focused on my skills and my process. I worked on my breath and repeated my affirmations.

This formula didn't just help shift my perspective; through it, I achieved one of my favorite accomplishments:

Seven fourth-quarter comeback victories in college.

It wasn't just about the victories for me; it was about rewriting the belief that I once carried. I went from "Can't perform in the clutch" to becoming "Cool Hand Luke."

But it all started by questioning the story I told myself after those early failures.

COMING UP CLUTCH

(PHOTO CREDIT: THE SPOKESMAN REVIEW)

THE PLAYBOOK

REFRAME YOUR BELIEFS

Return to your list where you identified the origins of your Inner Critic thoughts. Now ask yourself this:

Am I still letting a past performance define who I am today?

Was there a mistake, a loss, or a moment when you didn't rise to the occasion—and ever since, you've let that single event shape your identity?

If that's true, you're not alone. But now is the moment to challenge it.

Next to any Inner Critic thought that stems from a past performance or experience, write "(Past Event)" in parentheses. This is your way of naming the trap so you can begin stepping out of it.

Example:

- "Can't perform in the clutch."—Two missed game-winning opportunities in high school. (Past Event)

Now take it one level deeper.

Use the 3-Part Growth Formula to reframe that belief:

1. Outcome: What happened?
2. Learning: What did it teach you?
3. Application: What will you do differently next time?

Example:

- Outcome: Missed go-ahead throw in a rivalry game.
- Learning: I let fear of failure and outside opinions take over.
- Application: Next time, I'll stay grounded in my breath, focus on execution, and trust my prep.

This process helps you reclaim your story and remind yourself that one moment doesn't define your potential.

You're allowed to grow. You're allowed to evolve. And most importantly, you're allowed to win the next time.

"HAVEN'T DONE IT BEFORE"

"You can't write a book."

That thought hit me hard during the early stages of this project. Not because someone said it to me, but because I said it to myself. My Inner Critic was loud. Why? Simple.

Because I'd never done it before.

Sound familiar?

Athletes deal with this same thought all the time:

- "I've never played varsity before."
- "I've never started a game."
- "I've never performed well on a big stage."

And then the mind makes the leap:

"Because I've never done it, I probably can't."

But here's the truth: That belief isn't built on evidence. It's built on absence. It's all your perception and how you chose to look at it.

Think about it for a second. There was a time in your life where you hadn't:

- Taken a breath.
- Walked.
- Spoken.
- Read.
- Played a sport.
- Driven a car.
- Scored a point.
- Been a professional athlete.

The first time doing anything always feels awkward and uncomfortable. But uncomfortable ≠ incapable. It just means that you're growing.

So why do we let ourselves believe that "never done it" means "can't do it"? It all comes back to how we perceive events and the stories we tell ourselves. (Remember E + *P* + R = O? Event + *Perception* + Response = Outcome.)

Our story can either limit us—or launch us. And one of the most powerful tools to change your story is through **visualization**.

If you've seen the movie *Field of Dreams*, you probably remember this famous line: *"If you build it, they will come."*

Ed Mylett put a twist on it that I love:

"If you build it in your mind, it will come."

Each time you visualize yourself succeeding, leading, or achieving your goals, you're laying the foundation for those outcomes to become your reality. You see it before you live it.

Visualization is such a critical tool in my coaching. It helps the athletes I work with elevate their belief system and raise the standard for what's possible for them. Each time they see themselves succeeding, their internal success thermostat rises with them.

But most athletes don't use visualization—not because they don't believe in it or don't want to, but because no one ever showed them how.

I've been there.

I read countless sports-psychology books, learned about the power of visualization, and had a strong desire to learn, but no one taught me how. To help you avoid the same pitfalls I fell into, I want to give you some quick tips on how to visualize.

WHY THIS VISUALIZATION SYSTEM WORKS

Most athletes aren't bad at visualizing—they just haven't practiced it the right way.

Think about it: In school, we're taught to write. We're given time, space, prompts, and feedback. We're expected to do it and we're graded on it. So over time, we get good at writing—because we actually train it.

But when it comes to visualization? We're told it matters, but we're rarely shown how to do it. We don't get the reps. We don't get taught the structure. So of course, it feels awkward. Of course, most athletes say they "can't see it clearly" or "don't know what to imagine." That's normal.

That's why this system works.

We take a skill you've already practiced—writing—and use it to build a skill most people have never been taught. When you write the scene first, then hear it in your own voice, your brain builds the mental picture. Over time, those pictures get sharper. Stronger. Stickier. You're not guessing anymore. You're guiding yourself.

Step 1: Script the Outcome

Write down what you want to happen. Make it bold, specific, and present tense. Examples:

- "I *am* writing *The Mind Strength Playbook*."
- "I lead my team with poise and confidence."
- "I knock down the game winner and stay calm in the moment."

Step 2: Describe the Process

Write down how you want the process to go and how it feels.

- "I *am* writing this book with ease. The words flow through me. I know just what to say."
- "I feel calm and sharp on the field."
- "I'm in control of my breath and focus."

Note: For those players on team sports that have actual playbooks and play scripts for games or practice, this is a great place to write those play scripts down.

Step 3: Record the Script

Use your phone. Read the script aloud and record it. Add pauses between sentences to give your mind time to see it.

Step 4: Breathe and Play

Use 4-6 breathing (inhale for 4, exhale for 6) to relax. Once you're grounded, put in your headphones and play the audio. Let the visualization guide your mental reps. When your nerves start to rise during the visualization—and they will—breathe through them. It's the perfect opportunity to practice managing and utilizing them.

Step 5: Repeat.

You don't just visualize once and expect magic.

You visualize consistently—especially before big moments.

Pro Tip: Not letting your current reality limit what you write. Visualization is about creating what isn't real yet. Steve Jobs had to see the iPhone in his mind long before it existed. That's the power of vision.

THE PLAYBOOK

BUILD THE BELIEF

Look back at your list of Inner Critic thoughts and where they came from. Now scan for any belief that sounds like this:

- "I can't do that—I've never done it before."

- "I've never started, so I'm probably not starter material."

- "I've never performed well in that situation, so I probably won't."

These are not facts. They're stories you've made up based on a lack of experience—not a lack of ability.

If any of your Inner Critic thoughts fall into this category, write "(Haven't Done It Before)" next to them in parentheses.

Example:

- "I can't lead this team—never been a captain before." (Haven't Done It Before)

- "I'm not a finisher—never had the ball in my hands late." (Haven't Done It Before)

This helps you name the trap—and once you name it, you can start dismantling it.

Next Step: Visualization Reps

Choose one of the beliefs you labeled. Now walk through the visualization process from the previous section to start building a new belief around that exact area.

1. Script the success. What would it look like to show up with confidence in that situation?

2. Write the process. How does it feel when it's easy, fluid, and natural?

3. Record it. Use your phone to capture the visualization in your own voice.

4. Practice. Listen while breathing. Run the mental reps.

5. Repeat. Visualize consistently and make it a part of your routine.

Final note: When you visualize something you haven't done yet, you're laying the tracks for it to become real. You're training your mind to recognize it as possible.

You don't need proof to believe.

Belief creates the proof.

4. *Clear* Your Inner Critic

"It's not the snake bite that kills you—it's the venom that's left behind."
–Wayne Dyer

I remember listening to Wayne Dyer speak about the danger of holding on to emotional pain. He made this simple but powerful idea: "It's not the snake bite that kills you, it's the venom that's left behind."

That venom shows up as resentment, shame, guilt, fear, frustration—all the things we carry long after the moment has passed.

And here's the truth: We don't have a delete button in our brain. Events happen. People say things. We fail. We get criticized. And if we don't process those experiences, it's like stuffing golf balls into a garden hose. Eventually, the pressure builds, the water turns on—and there's no flow.

That's what happens when we don't *clear.*

WHAT IS *CLEARING*?

Clearing is one of the most important tools in my Mind Strength toolbox. It's a mental and emotional technique designed to remove the venom, unclog the hose, and free yourself to perform at your best.

At the heart of *clearing* is something most athletes don't expect—forgiveness.

I'll be honest, when I bring this up during a Mind Strength session, I usually get puzzled looks. Forgiveness? What does that have to do with mental performance?

The answer? Everything.

Because your energy is everything. And if your energy is blocked by resentment, fear, or regret, then it's not fully available to you in the moments that matter. You may be on the field, but your mind is somewhere else, and your focus, confidence, and freedom to flow will pay the price because of it.

HOW TO *CLEAR*

Clearing has two parts: external and internal. You can write them down or speak them out loud. Personally, I like to go for a walk and say them as I move.

1. *Clear* the External

This means forgiving the external world—people, moments, and situations that were out of your control.

Examples:

- I forgive my coach for the negative things he said to me in front of my teammates.
- I forgive the media for the criticism they threw my way.
- I forgive my parents for causing a scene and creating a distraction on game day.

Forgiveness doesn't mean that what happened was okay—you're not letting anyone off the hook. It simply means you're choosing to "*clear*" it from yourself, to stop carrying the weight and the venom.

2. *Clear* the Internal

This step is even more powerful: *Forgive yourself.*

This is where the true release happens. Because let's be honest, we are usually harder on ourselves than anyone else ever could be.

Examples:

- I forgive myself for letting that comment knock my confidence.
- I forgive myself for taking what my Youth Football coach said personally.
- I forgive myself for believing that I'm responsible for my parents' well-being.
- I forgive myself for holding onto doubt and fear.

Say it. Mean it. Let it go.

This is how you get free—not just mentally, but emotionally. And that freedom? That's where your best performance lives.

⅗ THE PLAYBOOK

CLEAR YOUR INNER CRITIC

Now it's your turn.

Take a look at your three Inner Critic thoughts you identified earlier. These thoughts didn't come from nowhere—they came from people, moments, and memories you may still be holding on to.

That's where *clearing* comes in.

This exercise is about freeing your energy so it can fuel performance, not poison it.

Find Your Space

Find a space to do this exercise. Choose something that brings you peace. My favorite way to *clear* is on a walk— somewhere quiet, no distractions.

Yours might be writing in a notebook or speaking aloud in your room. Do what works for you.

Start with External

When looking at your Inner Critic list, ask yourself:

- Who hurt me or let me down in this area?

- What moment or situation is still lingering in my mind?

Now forgive them. Out loud or in writing. Name it specifically.

Example (External): *"Not athletic enough to play quarterback."*

- I forgive my Youth Football coach for the hurtful things he said to me.

- I forgive him for never giving me the opportunity to play quarterback.

- I forgive him for playing daddy ball.

Say the statements with intention. Then take a deep, cleansing breath. Inhale peace. Exhale the venom. Visualize the weight leaving your body and mind.

Move to Internal

Now turn inward. This is where most of the venom hides. Ask yourself:

- What story have I made up about this?

- How have I held myself back because of it?

Forgive yourself.

Example (Internal): *"Not athletic enough to play quarterback."*

- I forgive myself for letting my Youth Football coach's words shake my confidence.

- I forgive myself for needing external validation.

- I forgive myself for any resentment I feel toward my Youth Football coach.

Pause. Deep breath. Inhale peace. Exhale the venom.

Keep *Clearing* Until It Feels Lighter

How long should you do this?

As long as it takes.

Some sessions may take five minutes. Some may go for an hour. Get in tune with yourself and you'll know when you feel it. Something inside of you will unlock and let go.

Just remember: *Clearing* isn't a one-time fix; it's a high-performance habit that requires practice.

You may have to revisit the same memory, the same pain, the same story multiple times.

That doesn't mean it's not working—it means you're human.

The more consistently you *clear*, the more space you create—for focus, energy, clarity, and confidence.

Clearing may be the single most important mental performance habit that you build. Because your mind isn't a trash can. It doesn't just have a delete button. You can't just stuff everything in and hope it all works out. If you want to be great, you must learn how to clear.

And the best part, *clearing* isn't just for athletes. It's for anyone who wants to give up resentment and release themselves. To let go instead of hold on. It's for everyone.

I joke with my wife sometimes that she's on my "*clearing* list," and we get a good laugh out of it. But the truth is, *clearing* is serious business. It's a phenomenal skill to help you *clear* your energy so you can be your best—mentally, emotionally, and spiritually.

5. Create New Thoughts

"A higher concept of yourself involves taking on new truths and shedding your old views of what you can achieve." –Wayne Dyer

You've done the hard work—identified the lies, traced their roots, cleared the emotional weight. Now it's time to step into truth.

Wayne Dyer called it "shedding old views and **taking on new truths**." That's exactly what this next step is about.

We're going to install new, empowering beliefs and rewire how you see yourself. How? Two words: *I am*.

"I *am*" affirmations are one of the simplest, most powerful tools in the entire Mind Strength Playbook. These aren't just positive quotes you tape to your mirror—they're declarations of identity. Each one, repeated over time, will help create a strong, confident belief system.

As Jerry Fankhauser put it: "Affirmations are like prescriptions for certain aspects of yourself you want to change"

We're doing just that: changing our old Inner Critic thoughts by replacing them with our new affirmations.

So let's write your new script.

"I *AM*" AFFIRMATIONS

There are three key elements that should be part of your "I *am*" affirmations.

A. Make It Present Tense

Words are powerful. The way we speak about ourselves shapes how we see ourselves. When you say, *"I am going to be strong,"* you're pushing it off into the future—like it's always out of reach. But when you say, *"I am strong,"* you're claiming that identity right now. You're speaking strength into your life in the present tense and allowing it to take root in who you are.

Avoid saying, "I will be confident!"

Say: "I *am* confident!"

Avoid saying, "I'm going to lead!"

Say: "I *am* a great leader!"

You're not wishing. You're claiming.

B. Make It Positive

You want your statement to be a strengthening thought that empowers you.

Say what you are: "I *am* explosive!"

Say what you do: "I *am* delivering under pressure!"

Remember: Strengthening thoughts → confident belief system → raises your internal success thermostat.

C. Make It Emotional

If it doesn't move you, it won't change you. You've got to feel it when you say it.

Like a coach told me once: "If it's juiceless, it's useless." It should spark emotion in you when you say it.

Examples From My Own Playbook:

Old thought: *"Not athletic enough to play quarterback."*

New affirmation: *"I am an amazing athlete and wow people with my playmaking ability!"*

Old thought: *"Don't have a strong enough arm."*

New affirmation: *"I am deadly accurate and make every throw on the field with ease!"*

Old thought: *"Can't perform in the clutch."*

New affirmation: *"I am Cool Hand Luke—I deliver in the clutch!"*

Each one of these checks the three boxes:

- Present tense? Check.
- Positive? Check.
- Emotional? Check.

🏈 THE PLAYBOOK

CREATE YOUR "I AM" AFFIRMATIONS

Take your three Inner Critic thoughts and rewrite each one into a present-tense, positive, emotion-charged "I Am" affirmation. This is how you raise your internal success thermostat.

Use the checklist to guide each statement:

- Is it present tense? ("I *am*," not "I will be.")
- Is it positive? (What you want to believe, not what you're avoiding.)
- Does it spark emotion in you? (You should feel something when you say it—confidence, pride, fire.)

Your turn:

1. Review each of your Inner Critic thoughts.
2. Flip each one into an "I *am*" that hits all three marks.
3. Write them down.
4. Speak them out loud with energy.

Avoid rushing this. This is you reshaping your identity—not just for today, but for the athlete and person you're becoming.

Applying Your "New Thoughts"

Congrats, you've done the heavy lifting to disempower your Inner Critic, *clear* out the lies, and *create* your "I am" affirmations.

Now the real work begins: applying it.

This is where most people fall off. They write down their affirmations once, maybe say them a few times—and then expect their belief system to magically shift. It doesn't work that way.

Belief doesn't form by accident, it forms by repetition.

If you want to raise your internal success thermostat, you've got to train it like any other muscle—daily, deliberately, and with intention.

THE PLAYBOOK

APPLYING YOUR NEW THOUGHTS

1. Write Down Your Affirmations

Each morning, put pen to paper and write down your "I am" affirmations. The repetition will help you memorize and internalize your affirmations. Do this before you check your phone.

2. State Your Affirmations Aloud

State your affirmations with emotion and conviction three times in the morning. Just like with writing them down, the repetition of speaking your affirmations will help you internalize them.

Pro Tip: Stack it with your workouts, right after your warm-up or between sets, when your energy and dopamine are high. Your brain is more receptive, and your body will feel the shift.

3. *Clear* and Affirm When the Inner Critic Gets Noisy

When your Inner Critic thoughts pop up (and they will), no panicking. Instead:

- **Acknowledge it.** Name the thought and acknowledge it for what it is: your Inner Critic. Being conscious of it is the first step to change.
- ***Clear* it.** Forgive both the external and the internal and let go of the thought.
- **Affirm it.** State your "I *am*" affirmations.

Remember, Mind Strength is a journey and a process, not a destination. It's not about perfection. We aren't trying to eliminate your Inner Critic. If I'm honest, I haven't figured out how to do that and I'm not going to pretend otherwise. What I have learned though is how to respond to it—how to stop letting it run the show.

And most important, how to be disciplined in it. Just because you did the exercise once doesn't mean your Inner Critic won't come back tomorrow. It's not enough to apply the exercise once; you need to apply it consistently.

I made this mistake my senior year before that dreaded Cal game. I let my Inner Critic thoughts go unchecked for too long. I let them affect my belief system and drag my internal success thermostat back down.

So avoid just trying this—train it.

Every day you show up to do these reps, you're not just building belief. You're building identity.

And every rep you run raises the thermostat a little more.

Handling a "Full Well" With Strength

Now, I'm sure some of you had this thought when we talked about "empty wells" earlier: **"Coach Falk, what happens when the well isn't empty? What if the feedback is coming from a credible source whom you respect?"** I won't leave you hanging on this.

The truth? It's harder. But it's just as important.

So how do you handle it?

By changing your perception and using the Mind Strength skills *"What, Not How"* and *"Clearing."*

Let me show you what I mean.

When I was coaching quarterbacks at Wingate University, we had 11 QBs on the roster. One of them, the guy dead last on the depth chart, came to me and asked why he wasn't getting any reps, then told me he wanted to play QB in the NFL.

I respected his dream. But as a coach, it was my job to be real with him. I had to tell him he was last on our Division II roster, with 10 other quarterbacks ahead of him, and that his chances of playing in the NFL were beyond a long shot.

That was a HUC conversation, what my dad calls a *Hard, Uncomfortable Conversation*. In these moments, I like to use what I call the **"hurt vs. harm"** filter. Yes, what I was about to say might hurt him, but it wouldn't harm him. It was for his highest good.

The alternative? If I stayed silent, he wouldn't have been hurt in that moment by my delivery, but he would have been harmed in the long run by me withholding the information I had.

Now once that delivery happened, this player could have taken it two ways:

He could've gotten defensive, hurt, and bitter about what I told him.

Or he could've leaned on me and my credibility as a coach. He could've allowed me to redirect his focus and energy toward a goal that was attainable for him.

It's the same choice you face.

When someone you admire tells you something hard, take an unbiased stance and ask yourself:

- Is there truth here?
- Can I use this to grow?
- Do I need to *clear* it, or is this feedback I need to face head-on?

After asking yourself these questions, you may find that even though the feedback is coming from a credible source, you disagree with them. And that's okay. Just because they are a credible source doesn't mean you have to agree with them.

This was the case with my old high school football coach.

I had two options: choose the safe path and go to Cornell, or bet on myself and go to Washington State as a walk-on. My coach strongly believed that Cornell was the right choice for me and that Washington State would never give me a chance. It would be a long shot.

And from an unbiased stance, he wasn't wrong. It was a long shot. He gave me sound, reasonable advice. But I disagreed and chose to bet on myself.

Going through the *clearing* process allowed me to forgive him for not fully supporting and believing in me, and forgive myself for being hurt by what he said. I released the venom, unclogged the hose, and allowed myself to play and live clearly.

I'll always remember the feeling of giving that coach tickets to my game against Oregon State years later, and knowing that he was watching in the stands as I threw six TDs in the first half and we cruised to an easy team victory.

So my advice: Listen to those who have credibility and you admire. But remember, you still get to decide what you will and won't give weight to. You hold the cards. The choice is yours.

Chapter 3 Review—
Reset Your Internal Success Thermostat

In this chapter, you learned that your belief system is the blueprint for your performance. If it's built on old stories, false limits, or unchecked self-doubt, it will cap what's possible—no matter how much talent you have.

But beliefs aren't fixed. They're formed. And anything formed can be re-formed. You've learned how to:

- **Recognize It Starts With Belief.** Start by examining your beliefs, because they shape your confidence, decisions, and ultimately your performance.
- **Identify Your Inner Critic.** Disempower your Inner Critic thoughts by identifying them.
- **Trace Their Origin.** Find out where your negative beliefs started and why they stuck.
- **Turn the Lights On.** Disempower the belief by "flipping on the light" and exposing the weak beliefs for what they are.
- *Clear* **Your Inner Critic.** Forgive, release, and free your energy to perform.
- **Create New Thoughts.** Build "I *am*" affirmations.

This is how you raise your internal success thermostat and make sure your mindset matches your goals.

Remember, Mind Strength is not a one-time fix. It's a daily decision to believe in the version of you that's still being built.

So keep showing up.

CHAPTER 4

Manage/Utilize Your
Game Stress & Nerves

"Pressure is a privilege."
—Billie Jean King

Friday Night Nerves

It's the fall of 2012, my senior year of high school. Through the walls of the locker room, I can hear our school's band playing a melody as the crowd starts to buzz in anticipation. Everyone is eager to see the small-town rivalry game. I sit on the bench lacing up my cleats, trying to steady my breath. But it's already too late. My heart's racing. Mind spinning. Stomach twisted up in knots. I jog out of the locker room and down a hallway in the Logan High rec center. There's a side bathroom there where no one bothers you. I shut the door and throw up my meal from earlier.

This wasn't the first time. At that point in my career, it had become a part of my routine.

Not because it helped, but because I didn't know how to handle my nerves. I let it build and overcome me to the point of puking.

And I know that I'm not alone in this. We all struggle with nerves. Maybe not quite to the point of puking, but we've all felt the dry throat and the racing heart. The knot in our stomach.

I've even had times where it was as if the nerves took control of my steering wheel and locked my ability to do the most basic things out on the field. It felt like I didn't have control. I feared that at any moment, they could rush over me and disrupt all the work I had put in.

And it wasn't until a mentor of mine shifted my perspective that I started to take back control. Instead of fearing nerves, I learned to embrace them and utilize them to help elevate my game.

My Perspective Shift

"If you change the way you look at things, the things you look at change."
–Wayne Dyer

Here's what changed for me:

If I changed the way I looked at nerves, the nerves themselves would change.

I used to look at nerves with fear and worry, but everything shifted once I took a more empowering perspective and looked at nerves as something that could help elevate my performance. With the right perspective, nerves could be a superpower. And it all started with the stories I told myself. (Remember $E + P + R = O$.)

The nerves (Event) weren't the problem. My perception of them was. I was assigning meaning to the butterflies, the sweaty palms, the churning gut. "I'm not ready." "I'm not in control." That story made me panic. So I responded by tightening up, second-guessing, puking pregame. And the outcome? I underperformed—or worse, unraveled.

But what if the story changed? What if, instead of resisting the nerves, you embraced them? What if you recognized that nerves weren't a negative, but proof you were about to do something you cared deeply about—and, as a bonus, they could help you elevate your game?

Here's what I mean…

In martial arts, there's a principle: Use your opponent's force against them. If they rush at you, don't resist—redirect. Use their momentum to throw them off balance. The same principle works with nerves. Instead of resisting the adrenaline spike, we can ride it. We can redirect it into focus, force, and freedom.

That's what I learned to do as a quarterback. In practice, there was a ceiling to what I could do. My throws had a certain cap on distance and zip. But in games, when I had my nerves working for me? I could throw 10 yards farther. My reads were sharper. My awareness tightened. Why?

Adrenaline.

The very thing that shuts some athletes down was unlocking a new level in me.

That's the key: When you shift your perception, you unlock a better response. And when you learn to respond to nerves with curiosity and control—not fear—you raise your performance ceiling. You don't just survive the moment. You compete freely in it.

Let's learn how to do that. Let's learn how to work with your nerves, not against them.

MANAGING GAME-DAY NERVES STRATEGIES

So how do we actually get your mind locked in, and use that energy to fuel your game.

- **Master the Cold to Handle the Heat.** Train your breath under game-day-like stress.
- **Find Your Pregame Zone.** Build a repeatable routine that centers you.
- **Clear the Pregame Clutter.** Release the mental clutter so you can focus freely.
- **Play the Game Before the Game.** Visualize the reps before they happen.
- **Prepare With Intention.** Trust your work by doubling down on what you control.
- **Turn Down the Noise.** Turn down the noise of the external world and tune in to your inner game.

Master the Cold to Handle the Heat

If you can master the cold in your training, you'll be able to handle the heat of competition.

You've heard me say it before—and you'll hear me say it again—your breath is everything.

What happens to your breath when you are nervous? It shortens and quickens. You breathe shallowly from your chest. Now think about when you're calm. Your breath slows down.

It deepens. It drops into your diaphragm. That's not a coincidence—it's a signal. Your body follows your breath. So if you want to change your state, change your breath. If you control your breath, you can control your nerves when they start to rise.

TRAIN YOUR 4-6 BREATHING IN THE COLD

Once you've built consistency with your 4-6 breathing (4 seconds in, 6 seconds out), it's time to level up. You're going to train your breathing in the cold—either a cold shower or a cold tub.

Why?

Because cold exposure mimics the exact reaction your body has when you're nervous before a game. Your breath gets taken away. Your chest tightens. So if you can learn to master your breathing in the cold, you'll be able to handle the heat of any competition. When you breathe in the cold, you teach your nervous system how to stay composed under stress.

Here's what happens with athletes I train:

- They learn to control their breath, even when it feels like it's being taken from them. This translates directly to those crunch-time moments on the field.

- They reframe the story they tell themselves during a difficult situation. At first, the inner voice is negative: "This sucks. I can't do this. It's too cold. How long do I have left?" That's the victim voice. But over time, with training, the voice shifts. It becomes focused. Process-driven. Confident.

- They build the skill of being present. I never tell them how long they'll be in the water. That uncertainty creates a mental challenge. At first, this causes issues for them. They focus on things they can't control, like when it will be over. But with training, there's a shift. The athlete focuses on the process, on things they can control. Their breath. Counting. They focus on the task at hand.

I've seen this carry straight over to game day. When the pressure's high and the chaos is swirling, these athletes don't get swept up in it. They slow it down. They find their breath. And they focus on the task at hand.

Take Bronson Evans, for example. Before our sessions, Bronson committed to 5 minutes in the cold tub. At first, it rattled him. He hated it. He had all the same thoughts most athletes do: "This is miserable. I can't do this."

But he stuck with it. He focused on his breath and not letting the cold take it away. He practiced strengthening thoughts like "I've got this. This is easy. This is helping me." His breathing got stronger. His focus sharper. He became a master at living in the present moment and focusing on the task at hand.

Descripton: Bronson Evans Utilizing Cold Breathwork Training.

THE MIND STRENGTH PLAYBOOK

That training came full circle in the Utah State Football Semifinals. Down 7. Nineteen seconds left. Fourth down. Everything on the line.

Bronson didn't panic. He didn't freeze. He found his breath. Locked into his skills. And delivered in the clutch.

Bronson delivered a perfect pass to tie the game, then continued his poised leadership into overtime, ultimately securing a thrilling one-point victory. This moment launched him and his team onward to become state champions.

Because he had practiced performing under pressure—again and again. When it came time to handle the heat of competition, he was ready.

(PHOTO CREDIT: ASTRONG PHOTOGRAPHY)

Description: Bronson Evans holding his team's State Championship trophy.

⚡ THE PLAYBOOK

4-6 BREATHING COLD TRAINING

Start small and continue to practice this exercise to build the muscle.

For the next week, add cold exposure to your daily routine. You can use a cold shower or a cold tub—whichever you have access to.

Week 1 Protocol

- Get in for 30 seconds.

- That's three rounds of 4-6 breathing (inhale 4 seconds, exhale 6 seconds).

- Stay focused on your breath. Stay in control.

Progression Plan

- Each week, increase your time by 30 seconds.

- Build up to 2½ minutes minimum.

- Most athletes work their way up to 5 minutes.

Mental-Focus Cues

- Control your breath. → Keep the cold from taking it away.

- Practice empowering self-talk. → "I've got this." "This is easy." "I'm in control."

- Stay present.→ Count each second in your head (1, 2, 3…).

⚙ COACHING TIP

4-6 BREATHING COLD TRAINING

Cold tubs are a great team activity for both physical recovery and Mind Strength training.

After our fall-camp practices in Lewiston, Idaho—where temps hit 95 to 100 degrees—Coach Leach had us pile into the cold tubs as a team. At the time, it was all about recovery. But it can be more than that. It can be a Mind Strength workout too.

Next time your players hit the cold tub, turn it into a rep for their mental game. Remind them:

- Control your breath—keep the cold from taking it away.
- Speak truth—"I've got this." "This is helping me."
- Stay present—focus on your breath and your count.

Done right, this becomes a shared moment of Mind Strength training—not just a break from the heat, but practice for it.

Find Your Pregame Zone

High performance isn't one-size-fits-all. It comes from knowing the state where you perform best—and mastering how to get there.

As you all can probably tell by now, I loved Tom Brady in high school. I wanted to be just like him. So I modeled my behavior after his. I watched him running out to Jay-Z's "Public Service Announcement," slamming helmets with teammates, screaming "Let's gooo!"

I copied him. The music. The hype. The energy.

I thought I was dialing into performance, but I was actually just dialing up my performance anxiety.

This didn't click for me until I read a book called *Mind Gym* by Gary Mack. He talked about something called an athlete's "number"—a kind of mental and emotional operating zone. Some athletes have a higher number and perform best when they're amped up and high-energy. Others have a lower number and play best when they're calm, centered, and composed. And if you are a low-number athlete trying to be a high-number athlete, you will only spike your pregame nerves.

This is what was happening to me. I was a low-number athlete trying to be like Tom Brady, a high-number athlete.

That insight changed everything.

Initially, "lower number" felt a lot like "less than" in my mind, especially when my idol, Tom Brady, operated from a higher number. So I started using language that made more sense to me: Amped or Relaxed. Not better or worse. Just different. Both can be elite.

And when I finally let go of trying to be something I wasn't, I unlocked a new level of performance. I stopped forcing hype and started finding rhythm. I became "Cool Hand Luke." That nickname wasn't just a persona—it was a Mind Strength skill.

Here's how to figure out your state—and build a pregame routine that works for you:

RELAXED STATE

Your goal is to lower your internal volume so your body and mind stay loose.

- Listen to calming music (xx's "Intro," classical music, John Mayer, etc.).
- Utilize your 4-6 breathing.
- Create space in the locker room—solitude, silence, prayer, or affirmations.
- Walk through your visualization mentally: calm, clear, focused.

This was the opposite of what I used to do. I used to blast hype music and bounce around the locker room trying to match everyone's energy. It spiked my anxiety. Once I learned to trust what I needed, my performance leveled up.

The xx's "Intro" became my go-to on repeat. I focused on my breathing, and I knew I needed space in the locker room to manage my energy levels before the game.

AMPED-UP STATE

Your goal is to raise your energy until it's sharp, not scattered.

- Play your favorite pump-up music (hip-hop, classic rock, heavy metal).
- Use energizing breath work (like Tony Robbins' "priming" routine) or move your body—jump rope, quick feet, push-ups—to increase your heart rate and get your blood flowing.

- Find teammates with similar energy and build the moment together.

Some athletes need a jolt to get in the zone. If that's you, lean into it. Build a pregame system that gets your heart racing and your mind focused.

Being able to dial in your pregame state is a critical Mind Strength skill that will help you utilize your pregame nerves rather than letting them handcuff you.

And remember, be honest with yourself about what best serves you. Just because your teammates are more "amped up" doesn't mean you have to be.

If you're relaxed, be relaxed. If you're amped, be amped. Neither one is better—only what's best for you.

Josh Allen once said he listens to Elvis Presley's "Love Me Tender" before games. That's his sweet spot. Calm. Grounded.[7] Tom Brady? He blasts Jay-Z. That's his charge-up zone.

Two elite quarterbacks. Two totally different states. Find your sweet spot.

THE PLAYBOOK

FIND YOUR PREGAME ZONE

Start with a quick self-check:

Are you more of an amped-up athlete or a relaxed one?

Most athletes I coach lean toward the relaxed side—but before learning this Mind Strength principle, they were unknowingly making things worse. They blasted hype music. They got caught up in the locker-room chaos. And it spiked their pregame anxiety instead of settling them into their zone.

Let's fix that.

Step 1: Identify Your Type

Ask yourself honestly:

- Do I perform best when I'm calm and grounded?
- Or when I'm fired up and energized?

Write it down: Relaxed or Amped.

Step 2: Build Your Pregame Plan

Now create a two- to three-step plan you can follow before your next game. Here's mine from college:

1. Listen to calming music (The xx's "Intro").
2. Practice 4-6 breathing.
3. Find solitude in the locker room to say affirmations and pray.

Write yours down.

Step 3: Test and Tweak

Run your plan before your next practice or game. Afterward, ask:

- Did it help me feel more in control?
- Was I in the right headspace to compete?
- What would I change next time?

Make small adjustments as needed. This isn't one-and-done. It's a process of refining your ideal pregame zone—so when the lights come on, you're exactly where you need to be.

Clear the Pregame Clutter

A cluttered mind can't compete. The strongest competitors are the ones who know how to clear the clutter, lock back in, and create space for their best to show up.

If you had followed me around the day before a game at Washington State, you'd probably find me alone in the stands at Martin Stadium. Or walking the field with my headphones in. I wasn't reviewing the playbook. I was *clearing*. I was talking to Janice Erickson, the coach who had been guiding me through *clearing* practices since the beginning of my Mind Strength journey. Why? Because *clearing* is a foundational practice—one I relied on as a player, use constantly in my coaching with clients today, and make sure to do for myself before any talk or big event.

You already learned the basics of *clearing* in Chapter 3—external, internal, and affirmations. That process is emotional hygiene. It's your regular maintenance, your daily reset.

But this chapter is about game day.

Game day is different. The stakes feel higher. The pressure intensifies. And so many athletes feel nerves, tightness, or hesitation—not because they're unprepared, but because they're carrying extra weight into the game.

It's that tough conversation from earlier in the week. The frustration with a coach or teammate. The doubt from a previous performance. A fight with a parent or partner.

It might not seem like a big deal in the moment... but when the lights come on, that stuff shows up.

In your body.

In your head.

In your performance.

That's why game day *clearing* matters. You've done the training. You've sharpened your skills. But if your mind isn't clear, you're playing with a weighted vest. The goal isn't perfection—it's presence. It's getting your mind clean so your body can follow.

⟨ẋ⟩ THE PLAYBOOK

CLEARING BEFORE A GAME

So how do you utilize *clearing* before the game? Follow these steps:

Step 1: *Clear* the Interference

Before a big game or performance, set aside 15-30 minutes. This can be done the night before or the morning of. Quiet space. No phone. Just you and the work.

Start with external: people or moments outside of you.

"I forgive Coach for benching me last week."

"I forgive my parents for distracting me before the game."

Then move on to the internal: the stories or tension you're holding.

"I forgive myself for needing approval."

"I forgive myself for the poor performance I had last game."

"I forgive myself for fearing and worrying about having a bad performance during my next competition."

"I forgive myself for the fear and worry of getting hurt or injured."

Say or write them. After every few, take a deep breath in, then exhale. Repeat until you feel lighter.

Step 2: Affirm What You Want

Use **"I Am"** and **"We Are"** statements to anchor the mindset and performance you want to bring into the game. They're mental blueprints. And when the nerves hit, they give your brain something clear and powerful to lock onto.

You can pull affirmations from Chapter 3—or write new ones based on where you're at this week.

For example, these are the ones I wrote down going into our Oregon State Game in 2016.

Description: My affirmations I wrote down & stated before our 2016 Oregon State Game.

That night turned out to be one of my best. And it wasn't magic. It was mindset—set with intention before the lights came on.

Clear the clutter. Then affirm who you are and how you're going to show up

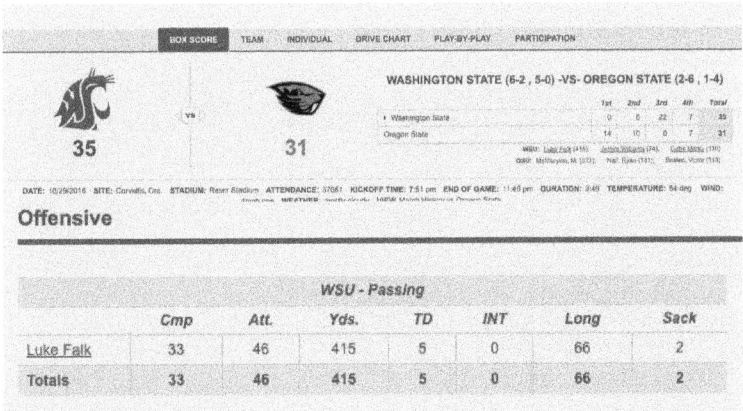

(PHOTO CREDIT: WSU ATHLETICS)

CLEARING IS A SPIRITUAL SKILL

This isn't just a mental reset. *Clearing* is a spiritual skill. Not religious—spiritual. It speaks to the part of you that holds emotion, story, fear, forgiveness, and peace. And just like physical or mental preparation, this part of your performance needs training too.

Most athletes don't realize how much clutter they're carrying—until it hijacks their confidence or focus. *Clearing* unclogs that internal pipeline. It frees your energy. It restores presence. It's not just mindset hygiene. It's spiritual clarity—and it's a skill you can master.

🏈 COACHING TIP

CLEAR THE CLUTTER

Coaches—this one's for you too. You feel the nerves before game day just like your players do. Especially if you're calling plays, managing the clock, or steering the strategy. If your energy is tight, your thinking will be too.

Use the *Clearing Method* as part of your pregame routine. Let go of the clutter. Get centered. You owe it to your team to be fully present and decisive. A clear coach makes better calls.

PARENT TIP

MODEL *CLEARING*

Got a big presentation? A stressful season of life? Feeling the weight of what you've been carrying?

Use the *Clearing Method*.

It's not just for athletes—it's a life skill. And when your kids see you model it, you teach them how to process emotion, release tension, and show up with clarity. Avoid letting your mental and emotional hose get clogged. *Clear* it. Be the example of what it looks like to reset and refocus. That's powerful parenting.

Play the Game Before the Game

It's a cold, wet October night in Eugene, Oregon. We're deep in the lion's den—Autzen Stadium—and the crowd is on its feet. The roar is deafening. I can barely hear my own heartbeat. It's third and 21 with 1:45 on the clock. We're down a touchdown. The ball's on our 19-yard line. I've just taken an 11-yard sack and missed a wide-open shot down the field. By every external metric, this drive should be over.

But inside, I'm calm.

That's the part people don't see. It's not because I'm fearless. It's because I've been here before.

Not just in practice. Not just on film.

In my mind.

I had played this game out over and over that summer. Quiet mornings. Headphones in. Eyes closed. I rehearsed moments just like this—crowds roaring, adversity mounting, the game on the line. I didn't just imagine it. I felt it. I breathed through it. I visualized how I would move, where I would throw, how I would respond. So when this moment came, I didn't need to get ready. I already was.

That's what visualization does.

It clears the noise. It settles the nerves. It allows you to feel the moment before you face it. So when it hits, you're not guessing. You're executing.

Yes, the stakes were real that night. Yes, the pressure was real. But I had already run that drive in my head—dozens of times. So when the pocket collapsed and I saw Dom Williams break open, I didn't flinch. I fired. First down.

And again, on third and 11. And again, on third and 12. And again, on fourth and 3.

And when we finally lined up with seven seconds left—no timeouts, ball on the 8-yard line—I took a breath, repeated my affirmations, lifted my leg, and trusted my training.

Touchdown. Tie game. One second left.

We won in double overtime, but the victory started long before kickoff. It started in the unseen hours—when I took time to mentally walk through the chaos so I could show up calm.

That's how you "play the game before the game."

THE PLAYBOOK

PLAY THE GAME BEFORE THE GAME

 You already learned how to visualize in Chapter 3. Now it's time to put it to work.

Go to your *"Virtual Locker Room"* and click on the "Pregame Visualization." I've created a version you can use anytime to mentally prepare and regulate nerves—before games, showcases, big events, or high-stakes moments.

If you want to level it up, I also do custom visualizations with my athletes—tailored to their sport, position, and goals. But start here. Feel the shift. And let it carry you into your moment, ready.

Because when your mind has already won, your body just follows.

Prepare With Intention

"Not preparing is preparing to fail." –John Wooden

Have you ever taken a test you didn't study for? Your nerves weren't just high, they were probably through the roof.

Now apply that to your sport. Game day is a performance. The lights are on. The pressure is real. And while you can't control everything—the score, the crowd, your coaches, your teammates—there is one thing you can control every time:

Your preparation.

Preparation is one of the most powerful tools an athlete has to manage stress and steady nerves.

I was listening to *The Herd with Colin Cowherd* when he asked Tom Brady if he got nervous before games. Brady said, "I always had nerves because it's a performance when you go out there on the field, and you would feel like you put a lot into it. There was anxiousness and nerves because the outcomes weren't guaranteed for any of us. The only way I knew how to combat the nerves and anxiousness of the game was to prepare."[8]

Brady knew that in order to perform his best, he had to prepare his best. He took the time to prepare throughout the week so he could go into his games with confidence. Same thing with Peyton Manning. His preparation and film study are legendary. Why do they go to these lengths? Because they wanted to walk onto the field on game day, knowing they did everything possible to prepare and perform their best.

It's no coincidence that when I was playing great football, I was on top of my preparation. I had a weekly game-week routine—outside of regular practice, lifting, and film sessions—that helped me prepare for the upcoming game.

Sunday (Day After Game)

- Recovery (cold/hot contrast, arm care).
- Film Study
  - Watch our prior game (utilize the 3-1 Tracker, coming up in Chapter 6).
  - Watch two of the most relevant games (full) on our upcoming opponent.

Monday (Player Off Day)

- Film Study
  - Watch opponent's first- and second-down cutups.
  - Watch opponent's explosive cutups.
- Recovery (cold/hot contrast, arm care).
- Mind Strength call with my coach.

Tuesday (Practice Day)

- Film Study
  - Review practice film.
  - Watch opponent's third down and red-zone cutups.
- Recovery (cold/hot contrast, arm care).

Wednesday (2nd Practice Day)

- Film Study
  - Review practice film.
  - Watch opponent's blitz tape.
- Recovery (cold/hot contrast, arm care).

Thursday (3rd Practice Day—Light)

- Film Study
  - Watch our pass concepts that other teams had run vs. our upcoming opponent's.
- Additional Football
  - Draw every play that was on our call sheet and put down the reads.
- Mind Strength
  - Visualize the play scripts vs. the opponents we were facing and my job and responsibility.
- Recovery (cold/hot contrast, arm care).

Friday (Walk-Thru—Day Before Game)

- No Film Study (Day Off)
- Mind Strength
  - Write down my affirmations.
  - Call for my *clearing* session.
  - Visualize the play script again.
- Recovery (cold/hot contrast, arm care).

Saturday (Game Day)

- Mind Strength
  - Manage my energy (relax).
  - Utilize 4-6 breathing.

On top of all that, every day I'd write down the three skills I wanted to focus on, run my breathwork drills, and use my 3–1 Tracker to lock in on improvement. (You'll learn this in Chapter 6.)

This prep didn't just reduce nerves—it gave me confidence. It made me feel battle-ready. The work didn't just start with the game week. My confidence came from consistently preparing during the offseason and knowing that I prepared to the best of my abilities.

Unfortunately, I didn't continue this routine when I got to the NFL. During the offseason, I didn't hold myself accountable or try to push myself to new limits. I didn't prepare. Instead, I enjoyed my new paycheck, along with a vacation or two. I allowed myself to get comfortable.

And when my moment came, I wasn't prepared.

That's the harsh part. They say luck is when preparation meets opportunity.

In college, I "got lucky" having my first career start turn into me throwing for over 500 yards and earning the Pac-12 player of the week.

In the NFL, I wasn't unlucky. It was the same scenario. Except the missing ingredient?

Preparation. When my opportunity came, I wasn't prepared to make the most of it.

Here's the good news:

This book, every chapter and every exercise, is helping you prepare for your competition and build the confidence to combat game-day nerves and stress.

👟 WALK-ON WISDOM

PREPARE THE SAME—"RESPECT EVERYONE, FEAR NO ONE."

"Respect Everyone, Fear No One."

That was another "Leachism" posted all over our football building—and it's critical when it comes to how you prepare and how you perceive the game ahead. When I was a college coach, we played a "lesser" opponent. Our QB had just come off an incredible run and had been named National Player of the Week a few weeks prior. This game though? He was... fine. Average.

From the outside, he played well. But he and I both knew it wasn't his best.

After the game, he pulled back the curtain:

"I overlooked this team. I didn't prepare like I should have."

He'd let the perception of the opponent dictate his preparation. He didn't respect them.

Fortunately, we still won big that day. But when I was a player in college, I wasn't so lucky. Twice I lost to FCS teams (yes, twice). The root cause? Walking into those games thinking, they're just an FCS team... not USC, Oregon, or Stanford. That mindset got us punched in the mouth.

On the flip side, you can't fear your opponent either. In my first career NFL start, we were facing the defending Super Bowl champions—the New England Patriots. The night before the game, one of our coaches, who'd been in the league for over thirty-five years, put up their defensive rankings (which I recommend not doing if you are a coach):

- First in Pass Defense
- First in Rush Defense
- First in Sacks
- First in Turnovers
- First in Points Allowed
- First in EVERYTHING...

Then he said, "Wow! I've never seen anything like this before!"

"Wow" was right. Not to mention they also had the greatest quarterback and coach in NFL history. We walked into that game, or at least I did, beaten in our minds before we even took the field.

So how do you protect yourself from falling into either trap?

Focus on what you can control.

In college, we'd get detailed scouting reports: "6'4", long wingspan, very fast, great hips—avoid throwing at him."

I stopped reading them. I'd just watch film and make my own notes. I focused on my job and responsibility. The beauty? Coach Leach didn't care about the external either. His philosophy: Do your job. Execute. Kick their ass.

It freed me from obsessing over certain players, conference awards, or NFL projections.

Most games, I didn't even know the names of the guys I was competing against until I'd see them drafted months later and think, "Oh yeah, that guy was pretty dang good!" There were a few exceptions, of course, like Vita Vea, Buddha Baker, Harry Gaines, and Harrison Phillips… Those guys were *damn* good.

This type of mentality was at the core of Leach's Air Raid philosophy and worked the same way. Stick to your identity. Run your stuff. Prepare the same, whether it's David or Goliath.

Respect Everyone. Fear No One.

Nobody's better than you, and nobody's less than you. Treat every opponent the same.

Keep your preparation the same. And focus only on what you can control.

⌀ THE PLAYBOOK

CREATE A PREPARATION PLAN

Map Out Your Weekly Routine

Take a few minutes to plan out what your ideal week of preparation looks like before a game or performance. Start with the day after your last competition and move forward.

You can use my weekly routine from earlier as a guide.

Pro Tip: Use what you've seen other top athletes do to get started—but make it your own. Adapt it to fit what you need and what works best for you. Be specific—vague plans lead to vague results. Build your routine with intention, not just imitation.

Design Your Offseason Plan

Your confidence on game day doesn't just come from game week—it's built in the offseason.

Use this same format to build a weekly plan for your offseason.

What do you need to commit to in order to build your mind, body, and skills?

Include:

- Strength and conditioning.

- Skill development.

- Mind Strength training
  (visualization, *clearing*, breathwork).

- Recovery and rest.

By writing this down and laying out a clear plan, you are more likely to follow through. I've experienced this in my own life. When I say I will do something but don't write a plan or my plan is vague, I don't follow through. Create a clear plan and have clear actions.

Final Check: Are You Moving the Needle?

Take a hard look at your plan and ask yourself:

- Are the things you're writing down actually helping you get better?

- Or are they just filling time?

Great performers don't confuse activity with achievement. They focus on what moves the needle. Pick the things that are truly going to help you succeed in your sport and aren't just things you are doing to pass the time. Build a plan rooted in purpose. Then show up and work.

"Don't mistake activity for achievement; practice it the right way."
—John Wooden

 COACHING TIP

LESS IS MORE. COACH FOR APPLICATION WHEN PREPARING YOUR TEAM

What Made Coach Leach Elite?

Coach Leach was a master of *application* and an essentialist at heart. It wasn't about how much he knew. It wasn't even about how much he could get us to know. It was about how much he could get us to *apply*. Because knowledge isn't power; rather the *application* of knowledge is.

Leach cut through the noise and zeroed in on what actually moved the needle. He didn't overwhelm us with everything— he focused on the few things that mattered and built systems around them. Too often, I see coaches overload their QBs. They can name coverages, fronts, and pressure rules... But they can't *apply* that information in real time. Coach Leach didn't coach for theory—he coached for execution. That's what made him elite.

So when you are helping your athletes prepare, cut the clutter. Focus on what matters. And coach/prepare your players to *apply*... Not just absorb and recite.

Turn Down the Noise

"Believing your own press clippings—good or bad—is self-defeating. You are allowing others, oftentimes uninformed others, to tell you who you are." –Bill Walsh

In 2015, I had a career year. In 2017, I had a season to forget.

2015 CAREER SEASON	2017 YEAR TO FORGET
Games Played = 12	Games Played = 12
Completion Percentage = 69.5%	Completion Percentage = 66.9%
Passing Yards = 4,566	Passing Yards = 3,593
Passing TDs = 38	Passing TDs= 30
Rushing TDs = 3	Rushing TDs = 0
Int = 8	Int = 13
Fourth-Quarter Comebacks = 4	Fourth-Quarter Comebacks = 1
Rating = 145.9	Rating = 137
Pac-12 First Team	Pac-12 Honorable Mention

In 2015, I committed to building my Mind Strength.

One of the biggest pieces of my protocol? The "No Media Rule."

- Deleted all social media apps.
- Didn't read a single article.
- Ignored rankings, opinions, and projections.

Result: Anxiety low. Performance high.

In 2017, I broke that rule.

- Kept social media.
- Read every article.
- Watched my rankings, our team rankings, NFL draft chatter—everything.

Result: Anxiety high. Performance low.

Why was my anxiety lower in 2015 and higher in 2017? Because social media is one of the most anxiety-producing products out there...

Think about what happens when you scroll:

- "How many followers do I have?"
- "How many likes did I get?"
- "What are people saying about me?"
- "Do I look good enough compared to them?"

Everything above is 100 percent external, 100 percent out of your control, and 100 percent guaranteed to spike your anxiety. Which is why social media management is part of Mind Strength training for my athletes—and for myself. If you don't put boundaries on it, it will eat away at your focus, your confidence, and your performance. Especially during the season.

I implement a "No Media Rule" with clients during competition periods. Simple rule: Delete the apps. No reading articles. Stay off the grid. Your job is to play—not to monitor what people are saying about how you're playing.

The game is already hard enough. Why make it harder by letting noise from the outside world hijack your mind? Trust me, when the season ends, the articles will still be there. So will the praise.

You're not missing anything permanent. What you *are* preserving is your mental edge.

BUILD THE MUSCLE BEFORE THE MOMENT

We don't wait until game week to start this discipline. In the offseason, we build toward it.

We track screen time. We take intentional breaks—what I call a "Social Sabbath." That might mean one day off a week. Or a week off per month. The goal isn't detox for detox's sake. It's to build the muscle of attention. Of focus. Of internal regulation.

Because once the lights come on and the pressure rises, you don't rise to the level of your motivation—you fall to the level of your training.

Start now.

Track it. Set limits. Experiment with breaks. Build the reps so when it's time to perform, your head isn't cluttered with the opinions of people who have no stake in your success. The game is hard enough as it is. Avoid piling onto this anxiety willingly.

🏐 COACHING TIP

THE "NO MEDIA RULE"

One of the highest ROI strategies you can implement during the season is the No Media Rule: Athletes delete social media apps. They don't check articles. They stay off the grid.

Here's why it works:

- Social media drives external focus—likes, opinions, comparisons.

- External focus increases anxiety.

- Increased anxiety kills performance.

The No Media Rule creates internal focus and mental clarity. It helps athletes stay locked in on what they can control: their preparation, mindset, and execution.

But here's the catch: FOMO is real.

The #1 reason athletes break the rule? Their teammates did. They feel left out, anxious, and disconnected. If even one player stays online, it weakens the discipline for everyone else.

As discussed in the bestselling book *The Anxious Generation*, peer-driven digital pressure is a major source of stress in high-performing youth. Remove the comparison trap—and you remove a major mental load.

Coach the standard as a team. Set the rule as a group. Frame it as a performance strategy, not a punishment.

You'll get buy-in, follow-through, and a locker room that's more mentally prepared to compete.

Chapter 4 Review—
Manage/Utilize Your Game Stress & Nerves

Nerves used to be the enemy—something to avoid, hide, and push down. But now? You've seen the truth: Nerves are proof that you care. And when trained, they become fuel.

This chapter wasn't just about managing pregame stress—it was about learning to meet pressure with presence. About owning your energy before it owns you.

You learned how to:

- **Master the Cold to Handle the Heat.** Train your breath under game-day-like stress.

- **Find Your Pregame Zone.** Build a repeatable routine that centers you.

- *Clear* **the Pregame Clutter.** Release the mental clutter so you can focus freely.

- **Play the Game Before the Game.** Visualize the reps before they happen.

- **Prepare With Intention.** Trust your work by doubling down on what you control.

- **Turn Down the Noise.** Turn down the noise of the external world and tune in to your inner game.

CHAPTER 5

Play the Next Play

"You have to have the ability to get past one play to the next, whether it's a good one or a bad one."

—Mike Leach

The Portland State Wake-Up Call

It's September 5—the opening kickoff to the 2015 season. Normally in Pullman this time of year, you're baking under 80-degree sunshine. But not today. Instead, it's 40 degrees, raining sideways, and the wind's got a personal vendetta. Not ideal weather for the Air Raid and a team trying to catch their footing. Not ideal weather for anything.

Still, we weren't sweating it. We were playing Portland State—an FCS team. Vegas odds had us winning easily. Or so we thought.

It's late in the fourth. We're down 24-17. Time's bleeding off the clock. It's fourth and 3, and we need it. I drop back—no one's open. So I take off. I spot a Portland State defender closing fast and, for some dumb reason, I think I'm going to hurdle him. Except I don't hurdle him—I get *launched*. My body flips. I land on my neck. My throwing arm lights up with a bolt of pain.

First stinger of my career.

But the physical pain wasn't as bad as seeing the final scoreboard.

Portland State: 24.

Washington State: 17.

And to make matters worse, the quarterback on the other sideline? He was from back home and played at the rival high school across town.

Ouch. Talk about rock bottom. Not only for me, but for my team and my university.

Cougar football opens with disappointment in loss to Big Sky's Portland State

Sept. 5, 2016 | Updated Sat., Sept. 5, 2016 at 6:35 p.m.

(ARTICLE HEADLINE: SPOKESMAN REVIEW) (PHOTO CREDIT: GREG & ASHLEY DAVIS)

I'll be honest—after the game, I was crushed. Mad. Embarrassed. Physically hurting and emotionally gutted. I sulked. I sat in it.

But later that night, alone with my dad, he hit me with a line I'll never forget. "Luke," he said, "success is all about how you recover."

The next day in the team meeting room, Leach stood at the front, arms crossed, voice even:

"We've got to play the next play."

Success Is All About How You Recover. Play the Next Play.

Can one play equal two?

Most athletes that I ask passionately disagree with me. The only players who seem to agree with the statement are my baseball clients, who joke that a double play could count as one play that equals two. But most push back.

But I say yes. One play can equal two. In fact, one play can equal three or four. It can equal a game. A season. Off the field, it can equal a day, a week, a year, a lifetime.

How?

If you allow the previous play to impact the current one. If you allow the baggage and frustration of a mistake to seep into the play at hand. Or even in your life, if you allow one bad moment to impact your day or let a bad week define your month.

Ask yourself: Have you ever allowed a previous mistake to negatively impact the next play? Have you let one play turn into two?

Here's the truth about high performers: they aren't perfect. Name any athlete who hasn't made a mistake. It's impossible. They don't avoid mistakes, they just recover faster than everybody else.

They're masters at the formula we've used throughout this book: $E + P + R = O$.

- The event happens—bad snap, missed shot, tough call.
- Their perception is clear, empowering, grounded.
- Their response is fast, focused, effective.
- The outcome? They stay in flow. They stay in the zone. They recover.

The average athlete gets stuck. They don't let themselves recover. They tell themselves a disempowering story and get caught up in the "Negative Play Cycle." (We'll go over this later on in the chapter.)

This chapter is about fixing that.

It's about building the mental muscle to play the next play—fast, free, and without the weight of the last one.

Because success doesn't belong to the perfect.

It belongs to those who recover better than the rest.

Play the Next Play Strategies

In this chapter, I'm going to give you the tools to play the next play and to help you recover and respond, just like your favorite athletes you watch on TV do. You'll learn how to play the next play when you:

- Understand the Impact of the past, future, and present moment.
- Understand the Negative Play Cycle.
- Learn from the Past
- Get Present
- Build Yourself Up
- Focus on Your Skills
- Be a Goldfish

Understand the Impact of the Past, Future, and Present Moment

Before we dive into the Negative Play Cycle and our Play the Next Play process, we need to understand one thing:

Where you place your attention determines how you perform.

That means understanding how the past, future, and present shape your mindset—especially under pressure.

Let's break it down.

THE PAST

You can't control it.

No matter how much energy you put into wishing things were different, wishing you could rewrite a mistake, change a decision, or take back a play, you can't. What's in the past is done. You can't control it.

If you let yourself live too far in the past—especially the negative stuff—you start to carry guilt.

"I shouldn't have thrown that."

"I let the team down."

"I knew better."

You start beating yourself up. And when that becomes your focus, guess what else goes up?

Your anxiety.

Why? Because you are focused on something you can't control.

THE FUTURE

You can't control it.

No amount of energy you put into obsessing and planning the future can guarantee the outcome you want. Nothing is promised. It's wasted time and energy.

If you live too far in the future—especially from a negative perspective—fear and worry will start to take over.

Fear for your health. Worrying about the outcome. Fear about the future. Etc.

And your anxiety? It increases. Why? Because you are focused on something you can't control.

THE PRESENT

You CAN control it.

When you focus on the present moment, right here and right now, you can control what happens. You can make decisions, execute, lead, and compete.

And your anxiety? It decreases. Why? Because you are focused on something you CAN control.

This is where peak performance lives: in the "flow" state or the "zone"—when you are totally present in the moment and not pulled into the past or worried about the future. It's that feeling when time slows down, the noise fades, and you're just playing— free, instinctive, locked in.

But it's not just for the field or court.

In your own life, living in the present is where you can experience peace and enjoy life at a different level. Away from the guilt about the past and what you didn't do, and free from the fear and worries of the future.

Understand the Negative Play Cycle

Now that we understand the impact of the past, future, and present, it's time to look at what actually happens when an athlete gets stuck in the spiderweb of the Negative Play Cycle, letting one bad play continue to impact future plays.

A negative play happens. A bad inning, a missed shot, a loss. And suddenly—you're not in the game anymore. You're stuck in your head.

Here's how it spirals:

YOUR FOCUS GOES TO THE PAST

You start replaying the mistake, wishing it didn't happen, and wishing you could go back and fix it.

You feel guilt and embarrassment.

You worry what your coach, teammates, parents, or fans think.

YOUR FOCUS GOES TO THE FUTURE

You start fearing the next play and worrying the mistake will repeat itself.

You're anxious about what might happen next—what people will think if it happens again.

Now you're not just carrying guilt—you're carrying fear too.

THE PRESENT PLAY IS IMPACTED

And with your attention split between the past and future, the present is completely hijacked. You're still physically on the field… but mentally, you're gone.

And what happens next usually looks like one of two things:

1. Timid Play

You play timid and scared, afraid to mess up and make another mistake. You stop playing to win and start playing not to lose. I've experienced this before. I got into my "Checkdown Charlie" mode and only threw the ball to my running back close by. I was too afraid to throw downfield.

2. Reckless Play

You play with reckless abandonment, trying to make up for the last play. It's as if athletes think that if they make a miraculous play the next time, it will be worth more points.

I've done this too. I threw three interceptions on back-to-back-to-back series. I tried to play hero and force the ball in an attempt to right the wrong from the first play. One play turned into three and I spent the rest of the game watching from the bench.

IMPACTS OF THE NEGATIVE PLAY CYCLE

- You are no longer fully present—your focus is split between guilt (past) and fear (future), and the current play is compromised.
- You fixate on the outcome, not the process—anxiety increases because you're focusing on what you can't control. Especially if you're concerned with how others view you.

(Outcome = Can't Control → Raises Anxiety)

How do you break this Negative Play Cycle and allow yourself to be present for each play, each series, each game?

You utilize the "Play the Next Play" Process.

The "Play the Next Play" Process

1. Learn From the Past

"No amount of guilt will ever undo what's been done.
If your past behavior mobilizes you to learn from your mistakes,
this is not guilt; it's learning from the past.

But to wallow in the present moment over your so-called errors is
guilt, and it can only take place now." —Wayne Dyer

As Wayne Dyer taught, there is no guilt if you learn from your past mistakes. In fact, this is the key to growth and experience. Compare a senior and a freshman for example. Even if they are equal in talent and physicality, the senior generally has the upper hand. Why? Because they've learned from their past. They have experience.

I'm sure we've all heard at one point or another the phrase "history repeats itself." Usually from a teacher trying to persuade their students that the reason we study history is to learn from it and ensure that we don't repeat the same mistakes. The same principle applies to your sport. If you want to grow, you've got to review the past—not obsess over it, but learn from it.

So it's not a bad thing to think about the past *if* you're using it to learn. That's the distinction. When you learn from it, your anxiety decreases. Why? Because learning is within your control. And now, that knowledge becomes fuel for the next play, series, match, or game.

It only becomes detrimental when you get stuck in the guilt—when you're just wallowing.

That's when anxiety rises. And worse, you miss the present moment entirely.

So how can you learn from the past?

In between plays, points shots, pitches:

- Self-reflection: What just happened? How can I learn from it?

In between series, sets, innings, holes, quarters:

- Self-reflection
- Coach feedback
- Teammate feedback
- Technology feedback (if your sport provides real-time film or stats)

Pro Tip With Teammates:

When taking advice from teammates, only drink from a "full well." During my playing days, I had wide receivers come up midgame telling me how open they were. The next day on film? Double coverage. Mental note made: not a reliable source. Make a mental note of the teammates who give you real, honest feedback that can help you. Listen to them. The others? Just gently nod your head as you are working on your 4-6 breathing.

In between games:

- Self-reflection
- Coaches' feedback
- Teammates' feedback
- 3-1 Tracker (You'll learn this in the next chapter)
- Study film

Pro Tip: Study the film, avoid just watching it like you would a movie. Analyze it and try to learn from it. What things did you do well? How can you keep implementing them the next time? What can you learn? What's your most valuable takeaway? What's one thing you can work on and apply next time? Too often, athletes are just passive spectators, but this gets you nowhere. Take an active approach and study the film.

THE PLAYBOOK

LEARN FROM THE PAST

Use this exercise to break free from past moments that still have a grip on your mindset. You're not just "moving on"—you're extracting the lesson so you can level up.

Step 1: Identify the Game or Event That Still Haunts You

What's one performance, one moment, one loss, one mistake you haven't been able to let go of? Think of a specific game or competition that triggers frustration, embarrassment, or guilt—even now.

Example: I had a hard time letting go of our game against the University of Washington during my senior year.

Step 2: Study the Game for Learning

Go back to that moment. Rewatch the film if you can. Replay the situation in your mind. But this time, you're not watching it to relive the pain. You're watching it as a student. What can you learn from it?

Write down two to three specific learnings.

My example: I learned that focusing on my skills—not the outcome—is vital to calming my nerves and getting into the right performance state. I learned that Mind Strength is a journey, and I have to apply it in every moment. It's not something I can take for granted.

Step 3: Reframe the Story

Now it's time to flip the narrative. What story can you tell yourself about that event that empowers you? What new meaning can you give it to help you move on and "play the next play"?

My example: That game was one of the best apprenticeships I ever had. It taught me how to build resilience and has become one of the most powerful tools I use now to coach others through their own turning points.

 PARENT TIP

RELEASE TO RESET

Struggling to let go of something from your past? Maybe it's a situation at work. Maybe it's a moment in parenting or your personal life that still lingers. If you're stuck there, the path forward starts with one powerful action: *Clear* it.

- **Forgive the External:** A person, a moment, a situation, even God—whatever or whomever you're still holding responsible.

- **Forgive the Internal:** Yourself. The story you've been telling. The resentment you've carried. The shame you hold. The difficulty in letting go.

This is how you release the venom. This is how you unjam the hose. Not just to "move on," but to move freely—with less tension, more presence, and parent from greater peace.

2. Get Present

"The ability to be in the present moment is a major component of mental wellness." –Abraham Maslow

Now that you've pulled the learning from the past, it's time to return to the present and break the grip of the Negative Play Cycle. Remember: When athletes spiral, their minds often leap from guilt over what just happened to fear that it's about to happen again. Their attention is no longer on the play in front of them—it's stuck in outcome-based thinking. That's where anxiety spikes and performance drops. Getting present is what breaks the cycle.

So how do you get present? Here are two methods I use. Both are powerful, but the first is especially effective in competition.

4-6 BREATHING

We've covered this earlier in the book for a reason—your breath is the fastest way to reset your system. When you count in your head—"1, 2, 3, 4" on the inhale and "1, 2, 3, 4, 5, 6" on the exhale—you're not in the past. You're not in the future. You're right here. Right now.

The same goes for feeling the rise and fall of your breath in your belly. This simple act of mindfulness puts you back in control. And that's why daily intentional practice matters—so you can access it in the heat of competition and pull yourself into the present moment and out of that Negative Play Cycle.

How to implement it:

- In between plays: One round (about 10 seconds).
- In between series, matches, holes, innings, or quaters: Three rounds (30 seconds).
- In between games: Build up over time from 1 to 5 minutes as part of your daily routine.

This is just a guideline. You know yourself better and how many rounds you need, so experiment and find your own sweet spot. Do some personal research and track what works for you.

GET IN TUNE WITH ALL FIVE OF YOUR SENSES

Our senses are one of the simplest tools we have to ground ourselves in the moment and fully live and enjoy life in the present. When you start drifting—whether it's guilt from the past or fear about what's coming—ask yourself:

- What do I hear?
- What do I see?
- What do I smell?
- What do I feel?
- What do I taste?

I learned this firsthand during a health retreat in Hilo, Hawai'i, when I was having a particularly hard time staying present. I was having some health issues, and my mind kept going to the future with fear and worry. "What if this is serious?" "What will happen to my family?" My mind and peace were hijacked by these fears, constantly pulling me out of the present and into a future filled with fear. My anxiety was through the roof. That's when Cindy, the leader of the retreat, gently brought me back with those same five questions. "Luke, What do you hear? What do you see? What do you smell? What do you feel? What do you taste?"

"I hear the birds and the waterfall."

"I see the markings in the wood ceiling above me."

"I smell lavender oils."

"I feel the warmth of the blanket."

"I taste the electrolytes I drank earlier."

Then she asked me: "In this moment, what do you have to fear?"

"Nothing."

That single moment reminded me how powerful presence can be. Getting in tune with my five senses helped pull me out of that rut. It wasn't a one-time solution, it's an exercise I had to practice consistently to build that muscle. And I still use this tool daily—not just in games, but in life. It grounds me in peace and helps me fully experience what's right in front of me.

Pro Tip for Competition:

While both of these methods are powerful, 4-6 breathing is the one I recommend in high-pressure, live-game environments. Here's why:

Let's say you're under the lights, crowd roaring, trying to get back in the moment. You ask yourself, "What do I hear?" and your answer is, "Falk, you suck! Bench him!"—not exactly helpful. Focusing on your five senses in the middle of the noise can backfire and trigger approval-seeking thoughts, putting you right back on that Teeter-Totter Trap.

But if you're in a quieter sport or environment without fans heckling you, your five senses might be the perfect entry point. Just be intentional and see what works best for you. And if you ask, "What do I see?" during a game, avoid looking at the scoreboard. That's outcome territory. Instead, find a focal point that grounds you, not one that pulls you back into anxiety.

PARENT TIP

STAYING GROUNDED

Want to help your child stay grounded in the moment? Start by practicing it yourself. One of the most powerful ways to model presence is through the simple discipline of tuning in to your five senses.

Next time you catch yourself drifting—worrying about the future, ruminating on the past—pause and ask yourself:

- What do I hear?
- What do I feel?
- What do I see?
- What do I taste?
- What do I smell?

Continue using this practice and, better yet, try it together. Take a walk as a family and turn it into a game: Each person names something from all five senses. It's a great way to take in the moment and live in the present.

COACHING TIP

INTEGRATE 4-6 BREATHING

Had a rough quarter? A shaky start to the half? Pull your team together and guide them through a round of 4-6 breathing to help reset their focus and bring everyone back to the present moment and the task at hand.

But here's the key: Avoid waiting until game day to introduce it. If you've never practiced this as a team, trying it in the heat of competition may backfire. Athletes can become self-conscious or disengaged if it feels unfamiliar or out of place.

Instead, make 4-6 breathing part of your regular training rhythm. Use it in warm-ups, post-drill resets, or even in film-review sessions. That way, when the pressure rises, your team will know exactly how to access this tool—and actually use it.

3. Build Yourself Up

"Being positive might not always work, but being negative always does."
–Jon Gordon

"You idiot, you never get it right. How could you be so stupid?"

Sound familiar? That's the voice of an athlete trapped in the Negative Play Cycle. But it's not just the tone that's harmful— it's the story underneath. That kind of self-talk is building a disempowering narrative. And as we've already learned, a disempowering story leads to a poor response, which leads to poor outcomes. Jon Gordon says it best: *"Being positive might not always work, but being negative always does..."* Just not in the way that supports high performance.

So how do we stop the negative spiral and start building ourselves up instead?

REPEAT YOUR AFFIRMATIONS

Speak life into yourself. My go-to during games?

> *"I am the #1 star player on this field!"*

> *"I am Cool Hand Luke–I deliver in the clutch!"*

These weren't just words, they were anchors I could return to whenever the imperfection of a game kicked in.

USE THE "CAN-DO MINDSET" SKILL

When doubt starts to creep in, repeat and tell yourself:

> *"I can, I can, I can, I've got this..."*

Or when it comes to your team:

> *"We can, we can, we can, we've got this..."*

CREATE A POWER STATEMENT

Make your power statement short, memorable, and, if possible, make it catchy by adding a rhyme or rhythm.

"I am Cool Hand Luke, as clutch as anyone has ever seen. I wow people with my plays and surely am the MVP!"

WHY THIS WORKS

I am a firm believer that your inner world drives your outer results:

Thoughts → Story → Words → Actions → Results

When your inner dialogue is strengthening, the domino effect starts working in your favor. And when it isn't? You already know the negative cycle that follows.

For me, the combo of affirmations and "Can-Do Mindset" was my one-two punch. I'd speak my affirmations before every drive. And when adversity struck midgame? That's when the "I can, I can, I can" rhythm would kick in.

This isn't fluff. This is mental muscle memory. And if you train it consistently, it will be there for you when you need it most.

 ## THE PLAYBOOK

CREATE YOUR GAME-TIME STATEMENT

Think of a powerful affirmation you want to embody—something that fires you up, centers you, and reminds you of who you are at your best. It should feel real, emotional, and energizing. For me, it was:

"I am the #1 player on this field!"

"I am Cool Hand Luke—I deliver in the clutch!"

Create your own affirmations for when you step into the arena. You can pull one from Chapter 3 in the "Out With the Old, In With the New" exercise where you wrote your "I Am" affirmations, or create a fresh one that fits your current mindset and performance goals.

Use the same three criteria:

- Make it present tense.
- Make it positive.
- Make it emotional.

Once you've got it, start using it. Speak it before a workout. Before a drive. Before a rep.

Train your mind to follow the rhythm of your belief. This is how you break the Negative Play Cycle and walk into every moment grounded in who you are.

I used to write "I Am" on my wristband before every game as a simple visual reminder to keep building myself up when everything else might try to tear me down.

(PHOTO CREDIT: WSU ATHLETICS)
Description: "I AM" written on my sweatband.

THE MIND STRENGTH PLAYBOOK

COACHING TIP

CREATE TEAM-INTENTION AFFIRMATIONS

Thoughts → Story → Words → Actions → Results

What we say becomes what we believe. And in a team setting, that ripple effect is amplified. When adversity hits—and it always does—that's when victim-minded athletes or coaches start slipping below the line. You need a way to hold the team steady. Here's a great tool:

Create Three Core "We Are" Affirmations

These become your team's mindset anchors—intentions you speak out loud, embody in practice, and fall back on when pressure spikes.

Why it works:

- It floods the environment with positive statements that create a positive story and lead to positive outcomes.

- It redirects their focus toward their statements and intentions instead of things outside their control, like the outcome.

Coach Leach lived this, even if he didn't call them affirmations. His intentions for us were:

- Be a team.

- Be the most excited to play.

- Be the best at doing your job.

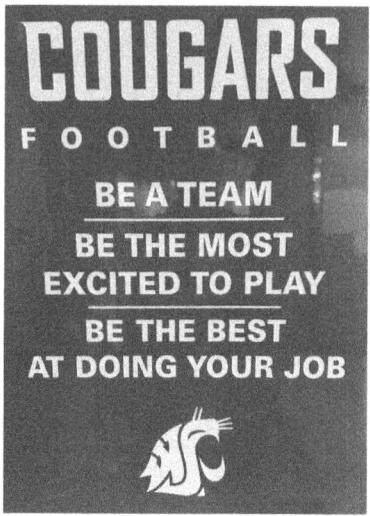

(PHOTO CREDIT: WSU FOOTBALL EQUIPMENT)

He hammered those into our heads every day. I believe they are even more effective if we turn them into empowering affirmations using the three building blocks we discussed earlier (make it present, make it positive, make it emotional).

Reframing Coach Leach's intentions:

- Be a team → We are a team!
- Be the most excited to play → We are the most excited team to play!

Be the best at doing your job → We are the best at doing our job!

Pro Tip: Make them part of your program's DNA.

- Say them in warm-ups, huddles, and postgame talks.
- Celebrate them in film sessions when players live them out.
- Redirect to them when players drift below the line.

They're not just mantras or some fancy cliche, they're identity markers. Live them. When a team knows who they are and repeats it daily, they stay grounded when the storms hit.

4. Focus on Your Skills

This is the final—and critical—step in the Play the Next Play process. It's the piece that breaks the Negative Play Cycle for good.

Remember what happens when athletes get stuck:

They go to the *past* and feel guilt.

Then they jump to the *future* and feel fear. And through it all, what are they focused on?

The outcome.

The result. The mistake. The scoreboard. The consequences.

And what does that do? Your anxiety spikes, your performance decreases, and the present play disappears.

So how do you shift your focus back to the moment? How do you stop obsessing over the outcome and lock in on the process?

You go back to what we learned in Chapter 2:

YOUR CODED SKILLS

Pick three skills that you want to execute during your competition. These will reset your mind and allow you to refocus, keeping you in the process and not focused on the outcome.

Think of it as your way to reenter the game with purpose and clarity.

To get the most out of this exercise, combine it with what we learned in step 1. Let's say this was the play:

Negative Play: I threw an interception on a vertical route to the left side of the field. (Yes, this actually happened… against UCLA in 2015.)

Learning: I need better eye discipline and make sure I get the safety to stay on his spot and not trigger on the ball.

Coded Skill: Eye discipline.

Now when I am refocusing my mind on the three skills I want to emphasize, I put the new learning into the equation:

- Eye Discipline
- Can-Do Mindset
- Be Decisive

That becomes my mental cue for the next play and helps me avoid repeating the same mistake. It allows me to refocus my mind on the process and not the outcome, ultimately getting me out of the Negative Play Cycle.

Be a Goldfish

"Coach Falk, Ted Lasso helped me add a skill today." That was the message I got from one of my athletes. I thought to myself, *This ought to be good*. I replied, "Yes? I can't wait to hear this."

He answered, "Be a goldfish—forget the bad things that happen and move on to the next thing. Ten-second memory."

I loved it.

That's the power of coding your skills and making them personal. He didn't just hear a clever line from a TV show—he saw a mindset principle that clicked. It helped him reframe the idea of moving on quickly and reinforced what we'd been working on: how to reset after a mistake.

For me, I've always called it "Play the Next Play." That's the language that resonates with me and keeps me locked in. But for him—and for many other athletes I coach—it's "Be a Goldfish." The label doesn't matter as much as the principle behind it.

Every great comeback in sports has this mindset baked into it. Whether or not it's written out step-by-step, the process is always there: Let go of the last moment, refocus on the current one, and respond with what you can control. That was true for me after the Portland State game in 2015. It was true for our team. And it'll be true for you.

The ability to recover is more than just emotional maturity—it's a competitive advantage. It's how you stay in the game, no matter what just happened. So whether you call it "Play the Next Play," "Be a Goldfish," "Flush It," or something else entirely, make sure you've got a code that brings you back to the present. That's where your power lives.

⚓ COACHING TIP

BE THE STEADY SHIP IN ROUGH WATERS

We were one of the best teams in the country when it came to fourth-quarter comebacks and game-winning drives. Why? Coach Leach was steady—unshakable. He played the next play and it rubbed off on us players.

I remember a game on the road at Rutgers. We had just lost the lead after going three-and-out, then gave up a punt return for a touchdown that put them ahead 34-30 with 1:18 left and 90 yards in front of us.

"Coach, what do you want here?" I asked, thinking he'd give me a play call. "Aaahhh… probably a touchdown," he said with a coy grin.

That's exactly what we got. (WSU 37 - Rutgers 34.)

Then there was 2016 at Oregon State. We were down 24-7 at halftime to a team we should've been handling. I walked into the coaches' locker room expecting adjustments and new ideas. Instead, Leach was on his phone… practicing Spanish. He looked up and said, calm as ever:

"There's nothing these guys are doing that's a surprise. Everything on our script I love.

Now go out there, cut it loose, and rip their ass."

To the team, he followed it up with a calm threat about holding a full scrimmage the next day if our effort didn't improve.

We went out and won 35-31.

Even when I was stuck in paralysis by analysis, he had the same approach. "Hey Falk, go sit over there and think about _____."

Now, I'm not going to say what the "blank" was… but it caught me off guard and broke my overthinking loop. He used that line with me for the rest of my career.

That was Leach—the Pirate. Calm. Unfazed by the big moment. I'm sure that same steadiness helped Graham Harrell, Michael Crabtree, and the Texas Tech Red Raiders in 2008 when they knocked off #1 Texas with one second left. I can almost hear him:

"Graham, just go think about _____ and score a touchdown."

So coaches, check your energy in the game, especially in big moments or when things aren't going your way. Your players will feel whatever you're putting out.

- Frantic? They'll feel it—and likely become it.
- Calm, composed, relaxed? That'll rub off on them too.

Be the anchor. Be like the Pirate. Play the Next Play.

Luke Falk comes up clutch to lift WSU over Rutgers
Sept. 12, 2015 | Updated Sat. Sept. 12, 2015 at 7:27 p.m.

Cougars pull double-overtime upset over Oregon
Sat. Oct. 10, 2015

Luke Falk named Maxwell Award Player of the Week
Thu. Oct. 29, 2015

 vs

45 **42**

WSU comeback makes Cougars bowl eligible
Nov. 7, 2015 | Updated Sat. Nov. 7, 2015 at 10:32 p.m.

Football | November 15, 2015 | Associated Press

Cougars Shock No. 18 UCLA In Final Seconds

WSU wins the Sun Bowl
WSU defeats Miami in the Sun Bowl, Saturday, Dec. 26, 2015.
Sat. Dec. 26, 2015

Mike Leach AP Pac-12 coach of the year; Luke Falk and Eduardo Middleton on first team

(PHOTO CREDITS: WSU ATHLETICS) (ARTICLE CREDITS: WSU ATHLETICS & SPOKESMAN REVIEW)

Chapter 5 Review—Play the Next Play

The great ones don't avoid mistakes. They recover fast.

That's the heart of this chapter. We learned what happens when one play turns into two, three, four—when the mind loops into guilt about the past or fear about the future. We broke down the Negative Play Cycle, and gave you a blueprint for breaking it.

Play the Next Play isn't just a mantra. It's a system.

You've learned how to:

- Understand the Impact of the Past, Future, and Present Moment.
- Understand the Negative Play Cycle.
- Learn From the Past.
- Get Present.
- Build Yourself Up.
- Focus on Your Skills.
- Be a Goldfish.

Every athlete—every person—gets knocked down. The question is:

Can you reset, recover, and respond with strength? Can you play the next play?

CHAPTER 6

The Falk Five: Core Mind Strength Skills

This chapter is a little different. I'm going to take you into five powerful Mind Strength skills and tools that every athlete, coach, and high-performer should have at their disposal. Ready? Let's go!

1. House Money

"More is lost by indecision than wrong decision. Indecision is the thief of opportunity." –Marcus Tullius Cicero

"Falk, stay here."

Leach's voice stopped me cold as the rest of the QBs filed out of the film room. I braced myself for what I thought was the inevitable a** chewing. Spring ball hadn't been going great. I was in the middle of a quarterback competition, and the guy I was battling with? A year younger, crazy talented, and truthfully, I was feeling the heat.

The season before in 2014, I'd ended the year as the starter after the senior QB got hurt. I'd played well enough to earn Pac-12 Player of the Week in one game, threw for over 600 yards in another.

"Falk, you've got to start playing with house money." I gave him a look.

"Think about it," he said. "If I handed you a hundred-dollar bill and told you to play at Zeppos," our little closet-sized casino in Pullman, "you'd play loose. Free. Like it didn't matter if you lost it."

But if it was your own hard-earned money? You'd tense up. You'd protect it. You'd hesitate."

Then he hit the core truth:

"Right now, you're playing like it's your own money—like you've got something to lose.

You were successful last year because you were playing with a walk-on mentality with no expectations and nothing to lose. You were playing with house money. Now you've put the pressure on yourself."

The light went on and everything clicked for me as he wrapped it up. "Cut it loose, be decisive, swing your sword."

That conversation was foundational for me as a player. I'd clawed my way into the starting job, and now I was letting the fear of losing it pull me out of my game. I was stuck in paralysis by analysis—second-guessing everything, trying to be perfect, overthinking my decisions.

Leach nailed it. "Falk, I'd rather you be wrong and decisive than right and indecisive.

Swing Your Sword!"

From that moment on, I had a new skill to anchor myself. *Play With House Money*. As a player, I used to call it *Be Decisive*. Leach had his own version: *Swing Your Sword*. But it all meant the same thing.

Let it rip. Cut it loose. Stop fearing the loss and start trusting your instincts.

This skill was crucial to sharpen my mindset during competitions and perform my best. It was the "Falk it" skill. When I executed on it, I was at the top of my game and unstoppable.

When I didn't? My kryptonite, overthinking, took over. The fear crept in, and the game tightened around me.

And it's not just me. One of the college QBs I coach now starts every coaching call with the same line: "Coach, house money again," as I asked him what was going well.

This skill works across every sport—tennis, baseball, wrestling, hoops, even rodeo. It's the John Wayne mindset. The "Falk it" mentality. The one that lets you drop the weight of everyone's opinions and just play.

Or, as Janis Joplin's famous song says:

"Freedom's just another word for nothing left to lose."

That's where you unlock your best. When you stop playing to protect and allow yourself to play free.

(PHOTO CREDIT: WSU ATHLETICS)

Description: Coach Leach coaching me during the 2015 Oregon game at Autzen Stadium.

⌐) THE PLAYBOOK

CODE IT AND CALL IT

Now it's your turn to take ownership of this skill. Give it a name that hits home for you.

That could be:

- House Money
- Be Decisive
- Swing Your Sword
- Cut It Loose
- Let It Rip
- Falk It
- John Wayne

Or something totally your own that resonates with you.

The key is this: Code it in a way that makes it stick. When you hear the phrase, it should trigger freedom, decisiveness, and the feeling that you've got nothing to lose.

Here's how to put it into action:

1. **Focus on it.** Choose your phrase and keep it front of mind during competition. Write it on your wrist tape. Put it on your locker. Lock it in before the game starts.

2. **Call it out loud.** When you feel the fear creeping in—the tightness, the second-guessing, the weight of "what if I mess up"—say your coded phrase out loud. Break the tension. Reclaim your mindset.

☞ COACHING TIP

GIVE THEM THE FREEDOM TO SWING THEIR SWORD

If you want your players to perform with confidence, to cut it loose, play with house money, and truly swing their sword, you have to give them the freedom to do it.

That starts with trust and consistency.

Too many coaches play the Jekyll-and-Hyde game. One minute, you're supporting your player; the next, you're ripping them out of the game for a mistake. You might think you're creating accountability or adding pressure to "toughen them up"—but what you're really doing is creating an outcome-obsessed environment.

And outcome obsession spikes anxiety and kills confidence.

Here's what happens: The player starts tying their value to every result. One missed throw? One turnover? One bad stretch? Suddenly they're on eggshells, playing not to lose instead of playing to win. Their mind shifts from process to panic.

I know because I lived it.

In 2015, I felt Coach Leach's full support. He even went on record saying I should've won the Heisman. I had a long leash—and I played free. That season, I cut it loose and performed at my best.

But in 2017, things shifted. Our relationship got rocky, and I started hearing the threats. I got benched more than once. The leash tightened. And my performance followed. I played hesitant. I analyzed instead of acted. I stopped swinging my sword. And it showed.

Now, to be clear, I didn't handle it perfectly. I let the outside noise impact my mindset. But as a coach, your job isn't to add mental hurdles during competition. Your job is to create an environment where your players can tap into their Mind Strength and compete at their best.

When I became a college quarterback coach, I remembered that. Once we named our starter, I told him: "The job is yours. I won't jerk you around." That player went on to become the conference's Offensive Freshman Player of the Year and even earned National Player of the Week honors after we upset a top-10 opponent.

The next season, I moved on to another job. That same QB. Same talent. But a different environment. Saw his completion percentage drop from 66 percent to 56.8 percent. Why?

Jekyll-and-Hyde coaching.

When I asked him what changed, he didn't hesitate: "I was afraid to make a mistake the whole season."

So here's the takeaway:

Fear of being yanked kills decisiveness. Create a system that allows your players to be bold. To fail without fear. To respond, not recoil, after mistakes. Correct when needed. Teach always. But stop yanking the wheel every time the ride gets bumpy. Let them swing their sword. Let them play with house money.

You'll like the results.

2. Grit, No Quit

"The greatest predictor of success is grit." –Angela Duckworth

If I'd come up in today's wild west of college athletics, I probably would've transferred after my first season at Washington State. I hate to admit it, but it's true. The combination of zero reps, no clear path forward, and the normalization of transferring might've pushed me to leave.

But back then? Transferring meant sitting out a full season or going the JUCO route. So I stayed. And in doing so, I learned one of the most valuable Mind Strength skills I've ever developed: *Grit, No Quit.*

Angela Duckworth, in her bestselling book *Grit*, studied the people who succeed—not just in sports, but across every arena of life. The most predictive factor? It wasn't IQ. It wasn't talent. It wasn't family income, education, or test scores. The #1 trait that determined success was grit. The ability to push through and persevere when others let up. To keep going when things didn't go your way. To stay focused on your mission, regardless of the circumstances.

That was me in the early years at WSU. Buried on the depth chart with the odds stacked against me. I had two choices: sulk or stay the course. I chose grit.

I took ownership and started getting creative. I met with coaches, studied more, stepped up my leadership, and actively looked for (and found) solutions. I didn't get distracted by the lack of immediate results. That's the grit mindset. It's long-game thinking. It's believing in delayed gratification in a world that's obsessed with now.

We live in a culture of shortcuts. A microwave society full of "quick fixes." AI gives us answers in seconds. Social media delivers dopamine on demand. And college athletics? It's become a revolving door.

But greatness doesn't work that way. Good things take time.

Grit is what keeps you locked in when the external reward hasn't shown up yet. And where does grit come from?

Your *Why*.

Your *Why* is your fuel. It's what pulls you out of bed when you're tired. It's what centers you when things go sideways. It's your anchor, your North Star.

Tony Robbins says, "If you have a big enough Why, you can handle any How." (Originally credited to Friedrich Nietzsche: *"He who has a why to live can bear almost any how."*)

If you have a reason that burns inside of you—a purpose that actually means something—you won't fold when adversity shows up. Because the fire is coming from within, not from what's happening around you.

So, what's your *Why*?

What's that mission, that dream, that deep-down fire that won't let you quit?

When you find it, and feed it, you'll discover that grit isn't something some people are born with.

It's something every one of us can build.

FINDING FUEL THAT LASTS

External motivaton is like rocket fuel. It explodes with power, it gets you off the launchpad, it jolts you into motion. But here's the problem: rockets burn through that fuel in seconds. If you don't have another source to sustain the flight, you either stall out or crash back down. That was me as a player—I was blasting upward on borrowed fuel, driven by the need to prove people wrong and to be seen. And like a rocket, eventually my tank emptied.

I wanted to prove people wrong. I wanted to prove my parents right. I wanted to feel like I mattered—like I was significant, whole, loved. I thought reaching the mountaintop would be the answer. Toby Keith's song "How Do You Like Me Now" was my theme during this time, playing in my head as I grinded, picturing the day I'd stand at the summit and finally feel seen.

And I did get there. I reached the mountaintop I had imagined. But it wasn't what I thought. I didn't feel whole. I didn't feel the long-term excitement. Instead, I felt empty and numb. My first thought was, *"If this doesn't make me feel good, then what will?"*

My motivation to stay at the summit was gone. My *"Why"* had gone up in flames. The gritty, daily routine it took to stay successful slipped because I'd unknowingly been climbing the wrong mountain all along—the external mountain.

When my playing days ended and I hit an identity crisis, I fell into the same trap. I tried to "save face"—to feed my ego and feel important again—by stepping into college coaching. Another mountain. Another summit. Another chance to feel significant. But again, it was built on the same shaky foundation: status, money, attention. I was chasing society's scoreboard all over again, running on cheap external fuel.

Then I got a wake-up call.

A family member received a life-changing diagnosis, and it forced me to stop and ask:

What really matters?

Now, with my clients, and with myself, I return to one powerful question:

---

*"Do I love the day-to-day grind,
or just the idea of the destination?"*

If you don't love the process, you're on the wrong path. You're just wishing time away, hoping "someday" or "somewhere" will make you happy. It won't. And in the process, you'll miss the moments that truly matter. That was me as a player—I didn't love the process. I didn't enjoy the film study, the practices, the meticulous effort. I liked what I thought the game could give me. And when I turned to coaching, it was the same story. I didn't enjoy the recruiting, the endless film, or the game planning. I was chasing the outcome, not the process.

That realization led me to call an audible. I pivoted. I still coach, but now I coach in a way that fuels me. I love helping people unlock their full potential. That's my fire. That's what I was made for. The rest? TikToks and recruiting pitches? That wasn't it.

Is there still some external motivation in me? Of course. I think that's part of being human. But now, the main fuel source is internal. It's rooted in living out my mission, not in chasing a scoreboard I can never win.

Here's how I see it. External motivation is like kindling: it burns hot, but it burns out fast. Internal motivation is the log: it sustains the fire over the long haul.

And when you stack the two together in the right order, you build a fire that keeps burning. The key is this: The primary source must be internal. **It has to come from within.**

✏ THE PLAYBOOK

CLIMB THE RIGHT MOUNTAIN

1. **List Your Burning Desires:** What do you want to accomplish? Be real. Be bold. Write them down.

2. **Write Out the "Why":** Next to each desire, go deep. What's driving you to want that? Peel back the layers. What's under the surface?

3. **Run the Ownership Test:** Ask yourself, *Is this desire truly mine? Or is it someone else's dream for me—parents, coaches, friends, social media, society?*

   - If it's someone else's? Cross it out. That's not your mountain. Stop wasting your climb.

4. **Check the Fuel Source:** Internal or External? Or Both? Label each desire:

   - Internal—it comes from within. (Example: "I want my driver's license so I can experience more freedom.")

   - External—it's about proving something or gaining approval. (Example: "I want to win Gatorade Player of the Year to shut up the doubters.")

   - Both—internal and external fuel. (Example: "I want to start because I love the game and I'm fueled by proving people wrong." If it's purely external? Cross it out. You're climbing the wrong mountain.

5. **Lock It In or Call an Audible:** If you're on the right mountain, keep climbing. When it gets tough, speak your *Why* out loud. Remind yourself: "Grit, No Quit." Let that line steady you when everything else feels shaky.

   But if you're on the wrong one—pivot. Call the audible. Realign. That's not quitting. That's wisdom. The strongest competitors aren't just relentless—they're aligned. So whether you're climbing or pivoting, do it with clarity and conviction.

3. State What You Want

"The mind can concentrate on only one thing at a time. So, rather than suppress what you don't want to happen, you must focus on what you do want to happen." –Gary Mack & David Casstevens

Think of a blue elephant.

What popped into your head? A blue elephant, right? Now DON'T think of a pink elephant.

Too late—what'd you picture? A pink elephant.

That little mind trick comes from Dr. Craig Manning. In one of our coaching sessions, he used it to hammer home a point I've never forgotten: Our brain quickly turns the thoughts we have into mental images; but the kicker is… our brain doesn't process the word "don't" the way we think it does. It hears the command, skips the don't, and builds a mental image around the rest.

So when you say, "Don't strike out," your brain generates a picture of—you guessed it—striking out. Same goes for the goalie who thinks, "Don't give up a goal," or the tennis player who mutters, "Don't hit it in the net." In each case, you're unintentionally rehearsing and visualizing the exact thing you're trying to avoid.

Dr. Manning's point with this type of exercise is when you tell yourself to NOT DO something or DON'T do something, you are actually programming yourself to do the very thing you are trying to avoid!

For example, if you are a basketball player and state, "Don't miss the shot," what mental image comes to mind? Missing the shot, right?

If you are a wrestler and say or think to yourself, "Don't get pinned," the mental image you create is getting pinned. The same can be said in football for a QB: "Don't throw a pick," which ends up being the mental image that pops into your head and programs you to do the thing you want to avoid.

You're programming failure.

Here's what you need instead: the Mind Strength skill I call *State What You Want*.

1. State what it is you want to happen (allow that mental image into your mind) vs. what you don't want.
2. Refocus on your skills and your process, not the outcome.

(Focusing on what you can control = anxiety decreases and performance increases.)

For example, if you're a golfer and you tell yourself, "Hit it in the fairway," then redirect your attention to what you can actually control: "Head down, straight front arm, 4-6 breathing," this combo—affirming what you want and focusing on how you'll get there—is what keeps you focused on the "doing" of your sport, not on the outcome and the anxiety that comes with it.

Now, I've got a buddy I golf with who shall remain nameless. He plays a lot—probably more than most—and he's got the physical talent to be really good. But every time we're out there, I hear...

"Don't hit it in the water." "Don't miss the putt." "Don't blade it."

Guess what happens? He hits it in the water. He lips the putt. He blades the wedge.

Why? Because that's the image he's rehearsing in his mind. Every one of those thoughts is focused on the outcome, not the process. Not on what he can control.

And when you focus on the outcome? Your anxiety spikes. Your confidence drops. And your performance suffers.

He's got all the talent in the world; but remember, *"Talent without Mind Strength is talent wasted."*

⚡ THE PLAYBOOK

HANDLING COACHES OR OTHERS TELLING YOU: "DON'T ____"

Can you control what other people say to you?

No. We learned that back in Chapter 1—other people's words are external, and external things are out of your control. And focusing on things you can't control is a waste of your time and energy. And almost always, an anxiety producer.

So, what do you do when someone says something unhelpful?

Picture this: A coach yells, "Don't turn the ball over!" or "Don't walk him!" or "Don't miss the putt!"

Here's where Mind Strength kicks in.

When someone gives you a "don't," flip the statement. Turn it into a clear, confident, "do."

Examples:

- "Don't turn the ball over." → "Take care of the ball."

- "Don't walk the batter." → "Throw a strike."

- "Don't miss the putt." → "I am sinking this putt."

- "Don't hit it in the net." → "I am serving it in play perfectly."

You can flip it out loud or silently in your head. Either way, you're taking ownership of your response and rewriting the script.

Once you've done that, follow it up with focusing on your skills—what you can control; the things you can do, not the outcomes you can't control.

Practice: Flip These

Start training this skill now. Look at the common phrases below—statements you've probably heard a hundred times. Flip them. Rewire them. Speak the performance you want.

- Don't be late.
- Don't screw up.
- Don't turn the ball over.
- Don't get injured.
- Don't hit it in the net.

Remember, you can't control what others say. But you can control your response.

State What You Want isn't just a game-day skill—it's a life skill. Once you start paying attention, you'll hear this kind of language everywhere. And most people? They have no idea the damage they're doing with their words. But you'll know better. And you'll perform better because of it.

COACHING TIP

STATE WHAT YOU WANT

Now that you understand how the brain works—how it doesn't process "don't" the way we think it does—start changing your language.

Avoid saying, "Don't strike out," "Don't turn the ball over," or "Don't mess this up." You may think you're protecting your athlete. But in reality, you're planting the exact outcome you're trying to prevent.

Your words become their mental images. Their mental images shape their performance.

So lead with language that builds, not burdens. *State What You Want.* Teach your athletes to do the same.

4. Deposit Discipline

"A journey of a thousand miles begins with a single step." –Lao Tzu

Every single day—with every decision—you're either making a deposit or a withdrawal from your goals, dreams, and personal standard. We tend to think greatness is built in big moments. But that's a myth. In reality, success is created through the small, seemingly insignificant choices you make daily.

I've heard this echoed by thought leaders like Robin Sharma, James Clear, Ed Mylett and Tony Robbins. But it hit home when I first read *The Compound Effect* by Darren Hardy.

Hardy defines the compound effect like this:

"Daily choices that compound over time, leading you to success—or disaster, depending on your choices."

It's simple but powerful. Every action is a choice. And every choice either moves you closer to success—or further away. Think of each one as a deposit (positive momentum) or a withdrawal (negative momentum) from your performance bank account.

Take a simple example: saving $5 a day. One day's worth? No big deal. But stack that daily habit?

- Month: $150
- Year: $1,825
- 5 Years: $9,125

Now flip it: Spend that $5 daily instead. That same compound effect leads to a negative balance:

- Month: -$150
- Year: -$1,825
- 5 Years: -$9,125

That's why the best financial minds call discipline the key to wealth. And it's the same with Mind Strength. When you see an athlete climb the mountaintop of success, it wasn't a singular big act but rather a series of small wins that helped get them there.

When I hit my stride at Washington State, it wasn't because of one moment or one practice. It was because I had stacked enough daily deposits—mentally, physically, emotionally—to cash in when the opportunity came. The process was consistent. And the results followed.

But during my final year of college and into the NFL? I thought I could produce the same outcome without the same input. I started making daily withdrawals from my preparation bank—and eventually, I emptied my account. The result? No success. Just a painful balance of regret.

SO, WHAT THINGS CREATE DEPOSITS?

These are the daily habits that pay you back:

- Mind Strength Training
  - 4-6 breathing
  - *Clearing*
  - Visualization

- Physical Training
  - Sport-specific drills
  - Weightlifting
  - Speed and agility training

- Mental-Sport IQ
  - Film study
  - Playbook mastery
  - High-level strategy

- Recovery
  - Nutrition/hydration
  - Sleep
  - Stretching, rolling, hot/cold therapy

WHAT ARE SOME OF THE BIGGEST THINGS THAT CREATE WITHDRAWALS?

Let's talk real numbers. Most athletes think they don't have time— but it's often not a time issue, it's a focus issue.

Social Media

Say you spend just 2.5 hours a day (below average for most athletes):

- 17.5 hours/week
- 70 hours/month = nearly 3 full days
- 210 hours/season (12 weeks) = almost 9 days of lost training, focus, and potential. When I break down this example for my clients their jaws drop to the floor. Why?

Because 2½ hours doesn't seem like that much time for them each day. Which it might not be. But compounded over time, it certainly is significant!

Video Games

Just 1 hour a day (which is below average):

- 7 hours/week
- 28 hours/month
- 84 hours/season = 3.5 full days

Combined?

- 24.5 hours/week
- 98 hours/month = 4 full days
- 294 hours/season = 12.25 days

That's *almost two full weeks* during the season of lost time that could've been invested toward your dreams.

Start asking yourself daily: "Is this helping me with where I want to go or is it limiting me?"

THE PLAYBOOK

DEPOSIT DISCIPLINE

You are your habits. They create your identity, your momentum, and your results—both good and bad. So let's get a clear, honest look at where your energy is going, and create a better roadmap moving forward.

1. List the Habits That Create Withdrawals

What habits are pulling you away from the person you want to be and preventing you from achieving your goals? Write them down. Be honest.

Examples:

- Social media
- Video games
- Poor diet
- Snoozing your alarm
- Skipping workouts
- Skipping Mind Strength training

- Negative self-talk
- Comparing yourself
- Quitting
- Victim thinking
- Etc.

2. Create a Countermove

Next to each habit, write a clear and specific action to counter or limit it. Avoid just saying, "Be better." Write down exactly how.

Examples:

- Social media ⟶ Set a 30-minute daily timer on your phone to limit social media use.
- Poor diet ⟶ Meal prep healthy food every Sunday.
- Snoozing ⟶ Put your phone across the room. Set multiple alarms.
- Negative self-talk ⟶ Practice affirmations before practice.

When your plan is clear, your follow-through increases. Vague plans = vague action.

3. List the Habits You Want to Keep

These are your current deposits. What's working? What's helping you grow? Keep them rolling.

Examples:

- Reading this book
- Showing up on time
- 4-6 breathing
- Journaling or visualization
- Hydration or recovery practices

4. Start New Habits

Now write the habits you want to start immediately. What's missing from your routine that would help you level up?

Examples:

- Going to bed earlier
- Drinking more water
- Practicing visualization
- Tracking nutrition or film study

Then write the "how" for each one.

Examples:

- Bedtime → Set an alarm at 9:30 p.m. to unplug and wind down. Keep a book by your bed.
- Water → Put a 20 oz. glass next to your phone. Drink it right after your alarm. Keep a water bottle with you.

5. Track It

Use a habit tracker. There are numerous apps available that let you track your habits—and even share them—for added accountability.

 Or scan the QR code to use the tracker in your *"Virtual Locker Room."*

⚷ COACHING TIP

LEADERSHIP DEPOSITS

Leadership can look a lot of different ways. There's no one right style, no one-size-fits-all method. But at its core, leadership comes down to something Coach Leach told me that's always stuck:

"Leadership is about elevating your group... getting the most out of the people you're leading."

That's the baseline. No matter what your style is, the job is the same: Lift your group higher. And there's a universal truth when it comes to leadership.

As Stephen Covey said, "You're either creating a "deposit" or a "withdrawal" with those you lead."

That's it. Every interaction you have with your players is either building trust—or draining it. And over time, those add up. Which leads to two kinds of leadership:

"WEALTHY" LEADERSHIP

Enough deposits made on a daily basis, compounded over time...

TRUST ⟶ BUY-IN ⟶ ELEVATING YOUR GROUP

"POOR" LEADERSHIP

Enough withdrawals made on a daily basis, compounded over time...

NO TRUST $\rightarrow$ NO BUY-IN $\rightarrow$ NO ELEVATING YOUR GROUP

If you want to build something that lasts—something your players believe in—you have to build it on deposits. Daily. Consistently.

I want to walk you through three points to help strengthen your leadership-deposit discipline—and create more trust, more buy-in, and ultimately, better performance from the athletes you lead.

Coach Effectively
(Coach Private, Praise Public)

"What the hell are you doing? You've f'd up this play five times now! You've got the dig!" That's what I was screaming at one of our wide receivers during spring ball heading into my senior year. And I kept going—for a solid minute. Did he absorb the coaching point? Not a chance. The only thing I accomplished was taking a massive withdrawal from his trust account. He shut down. His defenses went up. And whatever window I had to connect and lead? Gone.

That's human nature. When we're criticized—especially in front of peers or teammates—our walls go up. Our ego kicks in. And we protect. Too often, this is what coaching looks like. But it's not leadership. Leadership is about elevating your group. Getting the most out of the individuals you're leading—not shutting them down.

That receiver? He didn't lack physical talent. He lacked leadership from me. We never got on the same page that year. But the next season, with a new quarterback and a new voice in his ear, his game took off. He got drafted. The difference wasn't talent—it was deposits.

What I've learned—both as a player and a coach—is this: Coach in private, praise in public. That's one of the best tools you can use if you want to build trust and get results.

When you coach in private, defenses drop. Players aren't worried about saving face or getting embarrassed. They're open. Receptive. You're talking to the person—not the performance. And if you want to take it to the next level, use the Oreo Method:

- **First cookie layer:** Start with genuine appreciation. Name something they're doing well. Be authentic. If there's nothing real to praise, no faking it. Players can smell that a mile away.

- **The filling:** Deliver the coaching point. Be clear. State what you want—give them a mental image of the behavior or action they need to correct or apply. And most importantly, give them the tools to implement it. Knowledge alone isn't enough. Application is power. A great coach isn't just someone who knows—it's someone who gets their players to do.
- **Second cookie layer:** Close with the "why." Paint the vision. Help them see what's possible—what it unlocks for them and for the team if they apply the coaching. That gives the feedback purpose, not just correction.

That's the "Coach Private" piece. Now for the "Praise Public" side:

Catch them doing it right. Call it out. Highlight it. When you do, you're reinforcing exactly what you want more of. Most coaches only point out the negative—what's broken, what needs fixing. Sure, there's value in that, but it often comes from a fear-based mindset.

Instead, catch effort. Catch improvement. Catch execution. And then say it out loud.

Players want approval. If you shine a spotlight on the behavior you want, you'll get more of it. It becomes contagious. Players compete to earn praise, not avoid criticism.

This is how you build trust. This is how you make deposits. Coach in private. Praise in public. If you do, your players will play harder, grow faster, and believe more deeply—both in themselves and in you.

Follow Through on Your Word

I heard Ed Mylett say once on his podcast that one of the greatest confidence builders—or killers—is whether or not a person follows through on their word. That's not just about self-trust. It's about how people experience you, especially if you're in a position of leadership.

Think about someone you know who always says they'll do something but never does.

What's your confidence level in them? Probably low. Why? They've made too many withdrawals. And if someone's racking up withdrawals in their relationships, they can't lead effectively—no matter how talented or well-intentioned they are.

Now think about the opposite. Someone who follows through. They say it, they do it. You trust them because their track record says you can. They've made consistent deposits. That's the foundation of real leadership.

I'll be the first to admit—I haven't always been perfect in this area, especially in my younger years. And when I reflect on why I failed to follow through, it usually came down to two things:

1. I said yes to things I couldn't do—or didn't want to do.
2. I didn't schedule it.

I bet you've been there. You say yes in the moment to avoid letting someone down, but deep down, you know it's a no. And then you forget, get overwhelmed, or simply don't follow through. The result? Withdrawal.

One of the best tools I've found to fix this came from Brendon Burchard's *High Performance Habits*: "Say no in your head first."

Here's how it works. The next time someone asks you to do something, resist the automatic yes. In your head, say no first. This gives you space to ask two critical questions:

- Can I actually do this? (Check your schedule.)
- Do I want to do this? (Be honest with yourself.)

If either answer is no, your chances of following through drop. But if both are yes, you're greenlit—and far more likely to follow through. It's a simple but powerful filter.

Once you commit, write it down. Schedule it. Set an alarm. Create a reminder. Avoid relying on memory or good intentions. Even if your heart is in the right place, forgetting to follow through still registers as a withdrawal with the other person. As I heard a coach say one time… "The dullest pencil is sharper than the sharpest mind." Write it down. Use your calendar. Use your tools. There's no excuse not to.

Follow-through is trust in action. And trust is the currency of leadership. Keep your word, and your team will follow. Break it enough times, and they won't. It's that simple.

Get to Know Your Players on a Personal Level

Heading into my sophomore year at WSU, I was grabbing lunch with a mentor of mine—a former Cougar quarterback who had a successful career years before me. He gave me a piece of leadership advice that stuck:

"Get to know your teammates on a personal level. Do things outside of football with them." Simple. Brilliant. And it changed the way I led.

That year, we made it a priority to spend time together off the field—player-led activities, dinners, random hangouts, pool parties. No coaching staff. No practice script. Just connection.

And I believe it's one of the main reasons the 2015 team is still my favorite. We were tight. The culture was strong. And that group broke WSU's losing streak and helped get the program back to its winning ways.

That kind of connection doesn't happen by accident. It happens when players—and coaches—invest in each other beyond the jersey. It shows you care. It shows they matter. And it creates massive deposits in the trust bank.

So here's the challenge: Give them your time.

Have your players over for dinner. Introduce them to your family. Check in with them throughout the week—not just about football, but about life. Show them you see them as more than a position on the depth chart.

Because leadership isn't just about drawing up plays. It's about elevating your group.

And that starts with showing up for the people in it.

5. The 3-1 Tracker

"REFLECT ON YOUR PAST SUCCESSES. Every success, be it large or small, is proof that you are capable of achieving more successes."
–Napoleon Hill

"Learning to celebrate what is right about ourselves and the world we live in, is one of the most important mental skills I have learned."
–Dr. Craig Manning

After games, if you ask the average athlete how they did, you'll usually get some version of this:

"I should've done _____ better. I don't know what I was thinking there. I shouldn't have thrown that. I should've made that play."

Two things are almost always true:

1. They focus on the negative.
2. They focus only on the outcome.

That was me too—until I started working with Dr. Craig Manning, my sports psychologist. In his book *The Fearless Mind*, Dr. Manning introduces a simple but powerful mindset shift: Build confidence by tracking your previous performances.

"Confidence is accumulated when we learn and reinforce what we have done well in the past. Confidence and skill sets can be developed very quickly when we learn from our strengths." *–Dr. Craig Manning*

Most athletes never do this. When reflecting on a game or performance, they default to what went wrong. It's the brain's natural bias—to fix, correct, survive. But the best performers? They focus on what's going right. They focus on the small wins and learn from them. They study what worked so they can reinforce it and repeat it.

Here's what I mean: Imagine getting a report card with six A's and one C. Where do your eyes go? The C. You get down on yourself. Coaches and parents do it too—focus on the weak spot and miss the six things you did right. The result? You miss out on the confidence builder those A's could give you—and you miss the opportunity to learn from how you got those A's and how you could repeat it in the future.

My dad must've been ahead of his time. After my games, he wouldn't ask, "How'd it go?" He'd ask, "Luke, what were three things you did well?" This forced me to look at the positive rather than dwell on the negative. He'd then follow it with, "What's one thing you want to work on?"

It flipped the script. It pulled me out of the negative spiral and taught me to find the wins—even on my worst days.

When I started working with Dr. Manning, he took it to the next level. He used my dad's 3-1 approach but added a twist: Identify the skills, not the outcomes.

It wasn't "I threw three touchdowns." It was:

- *"I stayed in the fire."*
  I stayed calm and poised in the pocket and didn't flinch.
- *"I played with house money."*
  I was decisive and pulled the trigger.
- *"I had a great can-do mindset."*
  I consistently affirmed to myself, "I can do this, I can do this."

Three skills I could control.

Then one skill I wanted to improve.

- *"Win QB Math."*
  No negative plays. Get rid of the ball. No sacks.

That process became my personal performance review and research lab. I used it after every game, and eventually, every practice. It helped me understand which skills were allowing me to play at the top of my game and which skills I needed to build and develop.

We now call it the 3-1 Tracker, and here's why it works:

- It trains your brain to look for what's working—not just what's broken.
- It anchors your attention on skills and habits—things you can control.
- It turns you into a conscious performer—someone who actually knows what makes them good. (Which, by the way, is what separates great athletes from becoming great coaches in the future.)
- It lets you identify one skill to work on without falling into the guilt-and-shame rabbit hole.

This tool doesn't just help you feel better. It helps you play better. It builds awareness, confidence, and clarity—and it turns every game into a classroom for growth.

THE PLAYBOOK

MAGIC 3

Now that you've learned how to use the 3-1 Tracker, here's another tool I give to the players I coach. It's simple, but it's one of the most effective ways to identify the core Mind Strength skills that make you a great competitor.

Go back and watch one of your favorite games. Not just any game—a game where you were totally in the zone. A performance that still makes you smile when you think about it.

Maybe it was a game winner. Maybe it was a day where everything just clicked. Watch it.

Now take notes.

As you rewatch, identify three skills you were using that allowed you to perform at such a high level. Not the stats. Not the results. But the skills. The way you were thinking, behaving, and responding. What was going on between the ears?

For most athletes, when they do this, the same core patterns show up:

- *House Money*—"I was playing free. I wasn't worried about messing up."

- *Play the Next Play*—"I let mistakes go. I bounced back quickly."

- *Calm, Cool, and Collected*—"I stayed even. Didn't get rattled."

- *Can-Do Mindset*—"My self-talk was strong. I kept telling myself I could."

These are your core skills. They're the traits that unlock your best performance. Once you identify them, you can reinforce them and use them during your future competitions.

Pro Tip: Do this exercise, especially when you're in a slump.

My senior year, I hit a brutal stretch. We had that loss to Cal where I threw five picks and got sacked nine times. A few weeks later, I got benched in the first half at Arizona. Confidence was low. My energy was off. I was spiraling.

That's when my old high school basketball coach gave me a lifeline:

"Do you ever go back and watch a game where you played great? Just to remember what you're capable of?"

At first, I thought it was silly. Self-absorbed. But I was desperate. So I gave it a try. I added a twist, though—I didn't just watch to feel good. I watched to study. I wanted to understand what skills were showing up when I was at my best.

Here's what I found—my Magic 3:

1. **Can-Do Mindset**

2. **House Money (Be Decisive)**

3. **Cool Hand Luke**

Those three became my focus heading into our next game— Senior Day, my last game at Martin Stadium. We were facing #21 Stanford.

And here's what happened:

- Led a 94-yard game-winning drive in the fourth quarter.

- Capped off the first undefeated home season in WSU history (7-0).

- Broke the Pac-12 career passing yards record.

- Named Pac-12 Player of the Week.

That turnaround didn't happen by accident. It happened because I took the time to reset. To get back to the skills that made me me. This exercise helped me break out of the slump—and into one of the most meaningful games of my career.

So what's your Magic 3? Go find them. And next time you're off your game, return to them. They're not just tools—they're your personal blueprint to bounce back.

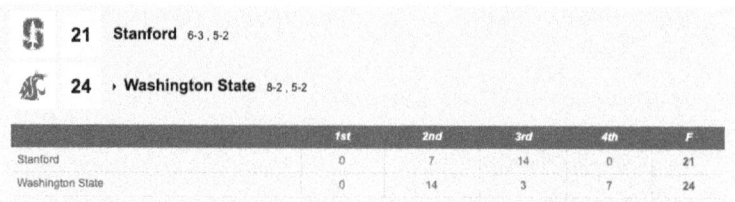

		1st	2nd	3rd	4th	F
Stanford		0	7	14	0	21
Washington State		0	14	3	7	24

Game Recap: Football | November 04, 2017 | By NICHOLAS K. GERANIOS

Falk leads No. 25 Washington St. over No. 18 Stanford 24-21

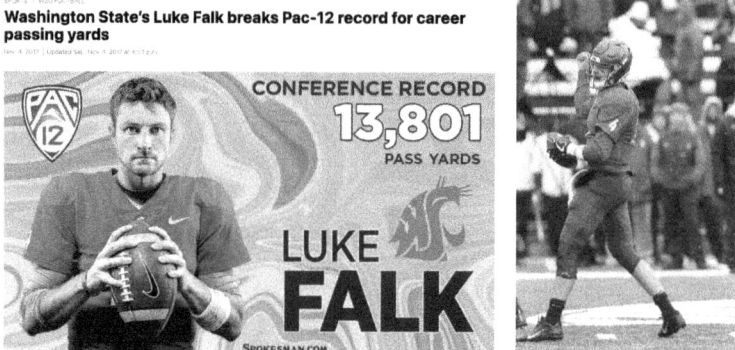

(PHOTOS CREDIT: WSU ATHLETICS, NICHOLAS K. GERANIOS, GREG & ASHLEY DAVIS AND SPOKESMAN REVIEW)

Description: Me after taking the final knee to beat Stanford 24-21.

 COACHING TIP

USE THE 3-1 TRACKER WITH YOUR TEAM

Start making the 3-1 Tracker part of your team's routine—after games, practices, scrimmages, or any competitive moment. Call out three skills the team executed well, then share one skill to improve.

Why? Because this simple structure helps your players build confidence the right way—by reinforcing the things they can control. It shifts the focus off of just outcomes and onto the process that created those outcomes.

It also creates a better learning environment. Your players start to look for their strengths.

They become more aware of what makes them good, and they get targeted reps on the specific skill they need to develop next.

Use it consistently, and you'll start to see your team's mindset evolve. Confidence goes up. Clarity improves. And progress becomes measurable. It's one of the simplest tools you can give them—and one of the most powerful.

PARENT TIP

USE THE 3-1 TRACKER AFTER GAMES

After a game, give your kid space to breathe. Let them decompress. Then, when the moment feels right, guide the conversation using the 3-1 Tracker.

Ask: "What are three things you did well?"

Help them focus on skills—not just stats or outcomes. Then ask: "What's one thing you want to work on?"

This approach does two powerful things. First, it builds their confidence by reinforcing what's working. Second, it keeps improvement simple and actionable—just one thing at a time. More importantly, it transforms the postgame talk from pressure to presence. From judgment to growth. And that's a gift both of you can carry into the next performance.

Chapter 6 Review—
The Falk Five: Core Mind Strength Skills

This chapter gave you something different. Not just one theme, but five essential Mind Strength skills—tools you can use across any game, practice, or pressure moment. These are the inner skills that separate good athletes from great ones. And they're now part of your toolkit.

You learned how to:

- **Play With House Money.** Cut it loose. Stop playing scared and start trusting your instincts. This mindset shift helps you perform freely and decisively when the moment counts.
- **Grit, No Quit.** Success isn't always about talent. It's about staying powerful. You built the skill of perseverance—anchoring your effort in your "why" so you can keep going when the road gets hard.
- **State What You Want.** You can't perform your best if you're focused on what you're trying to avoid. This skill rewires your language and thoughts to build positive mental images that drive results.
- **Deposit Discipline.** Every choice is either a deposit or a withdrawal. You built awareness around the small, daily habits that add up—and learned how to track and align them with your goals.
- **The 3-1 Tracker.** Growth doesn't come from obsessing over what went wrong. It comes from recognizing what went right—and what to improve next. This tool helps you build confidence and precision, one rep at a time.

These five skills aren't one-time tricks. They're lifelong tools. Tools to steady your focus, sharpen your execution, and elevate your game—on and off the field.

Keep them close. Keep them sharp. And when the pressure hits, you'll be ready.

CHAPTER 7

Create and Sustain
a Winning Environment

"Mike Vrabel, throw the f***ing ball!"

That's what I heard in the humid Tennessee night, slurred out by my mom and egged on by my uncle—both drunk, both loud enough to echo throughout Nissan Stadium. It was the fourth preseason game against the Minnesota Vikings, my first career NFL start, and a chance to prove I belonged. With none of the key starters playing in this game, the stands were mostly empty. And with both of them sitting in the front row, right behind the bench, every one of my teammates and coaches could hear the circus going on the sidelines.

I was embarrassed and distracted. My mind, which needed to be locked in and focused, got hijacked by the chaos happening 10 yards behind me. After the game, it wasn't much better. My parents were battling one another in a dragged-out divorce and a fight breaking out seemed inevitable. By that point, it had almost become routine. During my junior year at Washington State, after we beat Arizona 69-7 on Dads Weekend, I expected to be met with celebration.

Instead, I was met by cops. My dad had called them after my mom allegedly broke the "restraining" order he'd filed against her. It was unnecessary—and a total mess. Sadly, these kinds of back-and-forth theatrics were no longer outliers in the games to come.

But it wasn't just my family. The night before the Vikings game, my girlfriend at the time blew up my phone too, stressing about the anticipated family dysfunction she'd seen time and time again.

Was she wrong? Not entirely. But the timing? It was brutal. And it wasn't the first time.

All of it added up.

Looking back, this moment didn't mark the start of my fall. It was just the clearest symptom of it. I'd made it to the mountaintop—but I let the wrong voices inside the gates. The same hands that had helped me climb were now pulling me back down. And worse, I opened the door for them. My career didn't end because of a lack of talent. But the undisciplined environment I allowed around me played a role in cutting it short.

The hard truth? I chose it. I allowed it.

This mentality affected other areas of my life as well. Rather than surrounding myself with people pushing me to be my best, I had people contributing to the victim thinking that had consumed me. My motivation to do what I needed to stay at the top or get to the top was nowhere to be found. My lack of a clear "why" and the environment I allowed myself to be in held me back.

CREATING AND SUSTAINING A WINNING-ENVIRONMENT STRATEGY

This chapter isn't about blame. It's about ownership. And it's about protecting your potential. You can do all the training in the world. You can master every mental skill in this playbook. But if your environment is toxic—if the people around you drain more than they deposit—you will lose the war from within like I did.

Your environment impacts the decisions you make on a daily basis and shapes your behaviors. You can't be the best version of yourself consistently if you aren't in a great environment. Eventually, it'll break through the line and impact you.

Dr. Craig Manning framed it with a formula:

Potential+Training−Interference=High Performance

We've been working on your training. Your potential is already inside you. Now we need to tackle interference—and your environment is one of the biggest factors there is.

In this chapter, we'll break it down into three parts:

1. **The Core 5**—who you surround yourself with.
2. **The Intake Audit**—what you're letting into your mind daily.
3. **Your Inner Environment**—how honesty sets you free.

Let's build an environment that helps you rise—not one that quietly tears you down. Let's begin.

1. The Core 5

"You are the average of the five people you spend the most time with." –Jim Rohn

We take inventory of game film to see what we need to improve. We get grade reports to measure where we stand.

So here's the question: Why don't we evaluate the people we surround ourselves with?

Especially when your circle might be the most critical factor in whether you rise—or stay stuck. Just like you have a personal "success thermostat," the people around you carry one too.

And their setting doesn't just affect them—it affects you. Some people have a high temperature for your growth. They want you to win. They're comfortable watching you succeed, grow, and level up. These are your Core 5.

But others? They have a low success temperature for you. That doesn't always come with malice. Sometimes it comes with love, fear, or quiet insecurity. But here's the pattern: When you rise beyond what they're comfortable with—when you outgrow the box they've put you in—they start to pull you back. Consciously or unconsciously. Comments, drama, distractions, subtle shade, withholding support. You've probably felt it before.

In my experience, this pull-down effect almost always stems from insecurity—the fear that if you grow too much, you'll leave them behind. Or worse, that your growth exposes where they've stayed the same. Either way, the effect is the same: they become a weight.

You see this happen all the time in sports. An athlete has a breakout year, goes back home to visit, and ends up getting pulled into trouble by the same old crew. It's not that they're bad people—but their thermostat was set lower. And the rising heat made them uncomfortable.

I've seen it with clients too. After a huge game, they get texts from their girlfriend or boyfriend that aren't celebratory but accusatory, jealous, dramatic. Why? Because their success triggered something in the other person. That's not love. That's fear disguised as control.

Is that who you want in your Core 5?

Someone who feels threatened when you grow? Someone who reacts to your wins by trying to shrink them?

Here's one of the biggest truths I've learned:

Just because someone was in your Core 5 during one season of life doesn't mean they belong in this one.

I've got buddies from high school who were in my Core 5 for years. Brothers, really. But now? We've got different dreams. Different standards. Different definitions of "full potential." I still love them. Still see them from time to time. But the people I choose to spend most of my energy and time around? That's a different group now. One aligned with where I'm going in this season of my life.

Your Core 5 should reflect the future you want to live—not the past you're trying to outgrow.

PEER PRESSURE

When most people hear the term "peer pressure," they think of it as negative. But that's not true. Peer pressure isn't the enemy. It's actually neutral—it becomes either a deposit or a withdrawal based on who you're surrounded by.

Positive peer pressure is a powerful force. It helps you level up. It pushes you toward your potential. It's your group calling you out because they believe in who you can become. That's a deposit. That's alignment.

Early in my college career, this was my roommates and my teammates. We had a standard—and we all helped each other live up to it. We trained hard, stayed disciplined, and called each other on our crap. Not to tear each other down, but to make sure we were rising together. It was positive pressure—the kind that makes you better.

Negative peer pressure, on the other hand, is a quiet killer. It's peers nudging you to take shortcuts. It's subtle jabs at your discipline. It's people trying to make you feel like you're the weird one for keeping your word.

Example: Let's say you've committed to eating clean. Negative peer pressure sounds like, "Why are you being such a stickler?"

"C'mon, live a little."

Translation? They're uncomfortable with your self-discipline because it's shining a light on their lack of it.

Same with clients I've coached during their Social Media Sabbath week.

"That's dumb."

"It's not doing anything."

"Just redownload it real quick and check what I sent you."

That's not accountability. That's a withdrawal. It's influence rooted in insecurity—their discomfort with your progress gets projected onto you.

And here's the hard truth: You might be strong enough to resist that kind of pressure for a while. But eventually, if you keep swimming in that current, it will start to pull you under.

So how do you know which kind of pressure you're under?

Ask this:

- Does this group hold me accountable to my potential?
  - That's positive peer pressure. A deposit.
- Or does this group pull me away from my goals and mission?
  - That's negative peer pressure. A withdrawal.

Peer pressure isn't always bad. It just depends which direction it's pushing you.

BOUNDARIES

"Boundaries tell others where you end and they begin." –Dr. Henry Cloud and Dr. John Townsend

We know by now—you can't control other people. You can't control what they say, how they act, or how they show up. But you can control how you respond. And one of the best tools you have to do that is boundaries.

In their bestselling book *Boundaries*, Dr. Henry Cloud and Dr. John Townsend explain it like this: "Just as homeowners set physical property lines around their land, we need to set mental, emotional, and spiritual boundaries for our lives to help us distinguish what is our responsibility and what isn't."

One concept I love from their book is that healthy boundaries aren't walls. They're fences with gates. The point isn't to shut people out. It's to let the good in, keep the bad out, and protect your peace. Boundaries help you build a better environment— and take responsibility for the one you're in.

Unfortunately, I didn't learn that lesson soon enough. I tried to set boundaries, especially in college, but I didn't follow through.

One example? I told my mom that if she drank before or during my games, I wouldn't see her afterward. And I stuck to it—for a while. But eventually, I softened. I let the boundary slide. And as you saw in the opening story of this chapter, I paid the price. Not following through on a boundary isn't a small deal. It sends a message to others—and to yourself—that you don't really mean what you say.

If you're ready to take control of your environment, here are some boundary examples to consider:

Personal Relationships:

"No heavy conversations before a big game or an event. Let's talk after." "No unnecessary drama on game day—I need to stay focused."

Family:

"Give me 30 minutes after the game to decompress before we connect."

General:

"If you speak to me disrespectfully, I'm going to step away. That's not something I allow in my space."

Friends:

"I don't gossip or tear people down. I'm here to build, not bash."

Finances (especially relevant in today's NIL era):

"I'm on a budget—not a payroll."

"I'm not loaning or giving out money. I value our relationship too much to let money ruin it."

"If we go out, I'll pay for my own meal—but I'm not covering the group."

Pro Tip: Lending money always changes relationships. When athletes start making money, people come out of the woodwork. I had one friend ask me for money. I helped. Then he asked again.

And again. And again. Over time, I started to feel resentful. I felt used. The dynamic shifted, and it hurt a friendship that once meant a lot to me.

Eventually, I drew the line: "I won't be lending money anymore. I care about you, and I want to support you—but not like this." It was hard but necessary.

Remember, you hold the keys. You decide who enters your space and how much access they get. If someone repeatedly disrespects your boundaries, you don't have to blow things up—but you can create space. You can reward positive behavior and limit your exposure to negative energy. Boundaries aren't selfish. They're how you take care of your environment. And your environment will shape everything else.

 PARENT TIP

THE LINES ON THE FIELD OR COURT ARE A BOUNDARY

Growing up, my mom was notorious for yelling from the sidelines.

"Be aggressive!" "Shoot it!" "Luke, what are you doing?!"

What did that do to grade-school me? Did it help me focus on my game? Enjoy the sport? Not even close. I dreaded playing in games.

Then something incredible happened.

My parents went on vacation, and I had a basketball game. No pressure. No sideline yelling. No "Luke!!!" echoing through the gym. I scored 20 points. I played free. I actually enjoyed the game.

For the first time, I wasn't looking over at the sidelines after every play. I stayed locked into the game—not into trying to read my parents' body language.

And I know I'm not alone.

I've seen this dynamic play out again and again. Parents yelling from the stands. Calling out plays. Making scenes. It's become even more intense in the NIL era—where dreams of scholarships, stardom, and spotlight cloud what youth and high school sports should be about.

So here's the truth:

The lines on the field or court? Yes, they mark the rules of the game. But they should also serve as a boundary for you as a parent. Stay outside the lines—physically and emotionally.

Let your kid play.

Let them enjoy the game.

No interfering.

Your support means everything. But your sideline coaching? That might be doing more harm than good.

THE PLAYBOOK

AUDIT YOUR CORE 5

On the next several pages is a copy of the Core 5 Exercise for reference. Take a moment and review it here, then access it in your *"Virtual Locker Room."*

Read through the questions and think through the exercise first, then go and do it.

MIND STRENGTH **PLAYBOOK**

Mind Strength Exercise | Chapter 7

Core 5 Exercise:

Name:				
1				
2				
3				
4				
5				
6				
7				
8				

Step 1: Write down the names of the 5 closest people you spend the most time with. (Proximity)

Step 2: Answer the following questions:

1. Do I feel energized or drained after spending time with this person?

2. Do they challenge me to grow, or enable me to stay the same?

3. Do they support my goals and dreams—or subtly tear them down?

4. Are they living in alignment with values I admire?

5. Are they honest?

6. Do I become a better version of myself around them —or worse?

7. If I fully adopted their habits, where would I be in 5 years?

8. Are they genuinely happy for my success or are they jealous and resent it?

Core 5 Exercise:

Step 3: Ask yourself the following questions based upon your answers above:

9. Who do I need to spend more time around?

_____

_____

_____

_____

10. Who do I need to set boundaries with?

_____

_____

_____

11. If my performance, quality of life and mindset were the average of these five people would I be okay with that?

_____

_____

_____

_____

12. Are you somebody you would want in your Core 5?

_____

_____

Step 4: Apply what you just learned.

Now access this in your *"Virtual Locker Room"* by using the QR code.

🐚 COACHING TIP

ALIGNMENT IS EVERYTHING

In 2017, we had a split staff. Half were aligned with Coach Leach, and the other half seemed to be against him. One group accepted the quirks that came with working for Leach—him being late to meetings, his night-owl schedule, and his nontraditional football views. The other half resented it.

Had that resentment stayed internal, maybe it wouldn't have been detrimental. But instead, the complaining and blaming spilled over to the players—and unfortunately, I was one of the ones who listened to the wrong voices.

Listening to those voices fueled the fire of my 22-year-old immaturity and victim mindset, further driving a wedge between Coach Leach and me—the one guy who gave me a shot when a hundred other programs didn't.

In 2015? We were aligned.

I saw things the way he did. I bought in. I did everything I could to do my job and execute at the level he expected. I had his support—so much so, he even campaigned for me to win the Heisman. That season was magical. We had a special team, bond, and brotherhood that's hard to describe. What made it special was the alignment in the building. Coaches. Players. Staff.

Everyone pulling in the same direction. It was a "we," not "me" approach—and you could feel its power.

But as often happens with success when it's not handled effectively, it went to people's heads—mine included. Rather than the "we" being the focus, it became about "me." Coaches looked to boost their résumés, were quick to share disgruntled opinions with their position groups, and as a result, a fracture occurred. It showed up in the locker room and out on the field. A complaining cancer had been created—and it spread throughout the program.

New Buy-In:

Then in 2018, a fresh new crop came in. New coaches. New players. A new QB. New buy-in. That team was aligned—it was "we," not "me"—and they went on to have one the best seasons in WSU history: 11 wins and a season for the ages.

The Learning:

Looking back, it's a lesson I carry with me. Alignment is everything. Culture is key. And everyone plays a part in it.

One of our coaches once said that the lug nuts on a car's wheel are just as important as the high-powered engine. If they fall off, so do the wheels. A role that may seem small and insignificant can actually carry massive impact when compounded over time. Whether that impact is good or bad depends on the daily actions of that person and their level of buy-in.

If you're part of a team, you owe it to the greater cause to put pride and ego aside for the sake of the vision. A simple rule if you're an assistant, a player, or in any supporting role: Focus on what you can control. Don't like how things are being run? Create solutions and present them to the person in charge. Stop just bringing up problems—bring answers.

If your idea is accepted, execute it at a high level. If it's not, shelf it for when you're in charge. In the meantime, do your job and do it well. Complaining is a cancer. Avoid it at all costs.

Alignment is everything. Work to protect it.

PARENT TIP

JEDI-MIND-TRICK YOUR KID'S CORE 5

My wife always jokes that if she can just make something "my idea," I'll actually do it.

She's not wrong—and honestly, that's human nature.

Nobody likes being told what to do. Especially kids. That's why, when parents come to me frustrated that their son or daughter is hanging out with the "wrong crowd," I usually ask one question: Are you telling them, or are you helping them discover it for themselves?

Because here's the truth: Instruction isn't the same as influence. Telling your child what to do often goes in one ear and out the other. But helping them come to their own conclusion? That sticks. That shapes decisions. That builds discernment.

So instead of saying, "You shouldn't be hanging out with that kid," try asking questions that guide their thinking:

- "How do you feel when you're around them?"
- "Do you feel more focused—or more distracted?"
- "Are they helping you become the person you want to be?"

These kinds of questions are breadcrumbs—little clues that help your child start to evaluate their own environment and learn to trust their instincts. You're not just giving advice. You're giving them a skill to have greater discernment in their own life.

When your kids come to a conclusion on their own, the odds of real change—and follow-through—go way up. Because it's their decision, not yours. It's internalized, not enforced.

Great leadership is more than direction. It's preparation. So avoid just guiding them—equip them. Help them become strong enough to lead themselves. That's the goal.

2. The Intake Audit

"Stand guard at the door of your mind." –Jim Rohn

I saw a quote from Alex Hormozi that hit home:

"What you read, listen to, and watch is not entertainment—it's training."

He's spot-on. Every scroll, every click, every show, podcast, article, or video—it's all shaping you. Whether you realize it or not, it's training your mind. And over time, that training builds beliefs. Beliefs about who you are. What's possible. What to expect from the world. What to settle for.

In short, you become what you repeatedly expose yourself to.

So let's get honest for a second.

- Are you filling your head with fear-based news cycles that thrive on drama?
- Are you watching hours of "reality" TV that's anything but real?
- Are you numbing out on your phone, scrolling your life away?
- Or... are you feeding your mind with content that helps you grow?

With tools that sharpen your skills, deepen your mindset, and move you closer to the life you want? Because the truth is: Your environment isn't just people—it's also input.

And your Core 5 plays a big role here too. The people you hang with influence what you watch, what you read, what you believe is "normal."

So ask yourself this: "If someone tracked everything I consumed this week, would it show a person serious about becoming the best version of themself?"

That question stings a little. But it's a good one. Because every piece of content is either a deposit or a withdrawal. It either feeds your potential—or eats away at it.

If you want to elevate your life, start by elevating your inputs. Be disciplined with your content diet. Treat it like fuel.

And one of the best ways to stay consistent? A tool I learned from Tony Robbins: modeling.

We'll dive into that next.

MODELING

"Success leaves clues."–Tony Robbins

"If you want to achieve success, all you need to do is find a way to model those who have already succeeded." –Tony Robbins

Most people learn through trial and error. They take the long road. Mess up, adjust, figure it out eventually. With enough time and persistence, they can get where they want to go.

But there's a better way.

Tony Robbins talks about it. So did John Wooden, who said, "There's a quicker way to gain the information experience provides—ask somebody who already has it."

That's the essence of modeling.

Find someone who's already done what you want to do—and study them. Learn their mindset. Their routines. Their habits. Then apply what you learn.

In today's world, modeling has never been easier. With one search, you can find interviews, books, articles, training routines, mindset breakdowns—whatever you need. So let's make this practical.

HOW TO APPLY MODELING

Step 1: Identify a Role Model

Who's already where you want to be? Who's operating at a high level in your sport or field?

Pro Tip: Pick someone you respect holistically. A lot of people are "successful" in one lane of life but totally neglect the others. Avoid modeling someone who's a champion on the field but lost off of it. Find someone who's winning in all areas you care about—mind, body, relationships, and integrity.

Step 2: Research Relentlessly

How do they think? What are their daily habits? What systems do they use? What's their pregame routine? What are they reading, listening to, practicing?

Get curious and find out as much about them and what makes them successful so you can "model it yourself."

Step 3: Apply What You Learn

Start simple: Read the same books, follow the same routines, use their tools. You don't have to reinvent the wheel. You just have to get it rolling in the right direction.

Pro Tip: Focus on the needle movers. Ask yourself: *Is this habit, system, or mindset shift something that can really elevate where I'm at?* If yes, implement it. If no, move on.

And here's a wild idea:

Your role models can become part of your Core 5—even if you've never met them.

Thanks to today's tech, you can fill your ears with their words every day. You can study how they live, think, and operate. That's influence. That's shaping your environment in a way that works for you.

My Example: Tom Brady

I've probably made it clear—I admire and respect Tom Brady. To me, he's the gold standard of Mind Strength and competitive fire. So as a freshman at WSU, I decided to model my game, my daily decisions, quite frankly my life after his. So I began my process.

Every lunch break, I'd look up "Tom Brady" on YouTube. Interviews, training clips, whatever I could find. I read books. Took notes. Studied how he prepared, how he recovered, how he thought.

That's how I discovered *The Four Agreements*, which gave me two of my favorite tools: *"Take Nothing Personally,"* and *"What, Not How."*

I modeled him consistently. Built those behaviors into my day. And you know what?

It worked. Freakishly well.
Check this out:

TOM BRADY	LUKE FALK
Drafted: 6th Round Pick 199	Drafted: 6th Round Pick 199
Age 24 for First Start	Age 24 for First Start
Debut as Starter: Week 3	Debut as Starter: Week 3
Faced NFL Legend in First Start (Peyton Manning 2001)	Faced NFL Legend in First Start (Tom Brady 2018)

Description: Meeting Tom Brady after my first NFL career start vs. the Patriots in 2019.

The only difference that I didn't account for in this equation was that he played for the Patriots and I played for the Jets, and results showed...

Just kidding.

But here's the truth: I stopped modeling when I "made it." That was my mistake. I started strong—went to the TB12 facility, met with Alex Guerrero and the team—but I didn't stay consistent. I stopped doing the things that got me there. And it showed. Not just on the field, but in how I felt about myself.

So let this be your reminder: Modeling works—if you keep doing it.

If you're serious about your goals, stop just watching your heroes. Learn from them. And then apply. Daily.

⟫ THE PLAYBOOK

SUCCESS LEAVES CLUES: FOLLOW "ONE"

Modeling isn't just about admiring someone successful—
it's about putting their mindset and habits into motion in
your own life. Use this exercise to get clear on who you're
modeling and how you'll apply what matters most.

1. **What's the biggest goal or dream you want
   to accomplish?**

The one that burns hot. The one that lives at the front of your
mind. Example: Writing a bestselling book.

2. **Who is someone that has already done that—and who
   you respect holistically?**

Make sure it's someone who doesn't just have the outcome,
but lives the kind of life you want.

Example: Ed Mylett.

3. **What are some characteristics this person
   displays that you admire?**

No overthinking it. Just list what stands out. Example:

- Courageous
- Vulnerable
- Walks the walk
- Honest
- Disciplined

4. **Circle the ONE characteristic you most want
   to embody right now.**

The one that, if it became part of how you live, would help
move the needle most. Example: Walk the walk.

5. Apply it.

Start showing up today like someone who lives that value. You can't control the outcome, but you can control your character. If you model the mindset and habits of someone who's already climbed the mountain, you'll give yourself a real shot at reaching the summit too.

COACHING TIP

LIVE YOUR COACHING: BE THE MODEL, NOT JUST THE VOICE

"It is no use walking anywhere to preach unless our walking is our preaching." —St. Francis of Assisi

Ask yourself this simple but revealing question: Would you want your players to model their behavior after yours?

If the answer is no, something's off. If the answer is yes, double down.

- You want discipline from your players? Be disciplined.
- You want respect from your players? Give respect.
- You want commitment? Live it.

Too often, coaching becomes a one-way street. A "Do as I say, not as I do" approach. But here's the truth: Players can smell inauthenticity. If you lack follow-through in your own routine but demand it from them, they'll check out. If you bark orders but don't walk your own talk, you'll lose the locker room.

Start living your coaching. Start being the model.

"What you do has far greater impact than what you say."
—Stephen R. Covey

3. Your Inner Environment

"If you tell the truth, you don't have to remember anything."
—Mark Twain

Protecting your environment isn't just about who and what you let in—it's also about the honesty you live with inside yourself. If you aren't honest with yourself or others, your inner environment and foundation begin to suffer. Little by little, each lie becomes a weight that interferes with your performance, your mental state, your conscience, and your peace. I've experienced this firsthand.

🥾 WALK-ON WISDOM

PASS THE PILLOW TEST

If I were asked what is one regret I have, it would be this:

I wasn't honest in my younger years.

We're wired to move toward what feels good and avoid what feels painful. For me, lying became a shield—a way to protect myself from the potential pain I feared would come from rejection, from not being accepted, from not being loved.

I've battled insecurity for much of my life, carrying the weight of feeling "not good enough." I often wished I were different; different talents, a different body, different circumstances.

That insecurity led to a lack of honesty. I said what I thought people wanted to hear and avoided vulnerability out of fear they wouldn't accept the real me. My self-worth became tied to being liked and accepted.

Especially early on in personal relationships, I'd tell stories. And the thing about stories is—you have to remember them. That creates a mental weight. Little by little, it becomes a source of interference. It wears you down.

Honesty is a Mind Strength skill. It's not only about being truthful with others. It's about shaping an inner environment where peace can actually live. Without that, no outer environment will ever feel right. It brings peace. It mitigates interference. It gives you a clean conscience. It helps you pass the pillow test at night, knowing you did your best.

But here's the truth: Without honesty, you can't truly grow. If you're lying to yourself or others, everything you build will be tainted. Honesty requires you to be okay with discomfort. It demands vulnerability. It means accepting the possibility of rejection. And to do that—you have to love yourself.

I believe the greatest Mind Strength skill you can ever develop is self-love.

It's the foundation of a beautiful life. It's the key to inner mastery. It's at the core of Mind Strength.

The moments in my life when I've truly loved and accepted myself are the moments the handcuffs of anxiety come off, the need to be someone I'm not disappears, honesty becomes my foundation, and the thing we're all searching for sets in—peace.

Peace doesn't come from pretending to be something you're not. It comes from choosing honesty, embracing who you are, and loving yourself through it all. You must be honest with yourself and those around you.

A guiding principle that has helped me on this self-love journey is one I learned in 2020 during an Al-Anon meeting: the Serenity Prayer.

"God, grant me the serenity to accept the things I cannot change, courage to change the things I can, and wisdom to know the difference."

From the Serenity Prayer, a powerful spiritual Mind Strength skill is created: *acceptance*.

Acceptance for the things you cannot change—your talents, your circumstances, your body, the future, the past, or what others say and do. It all comes back to controlling what you can. It's about receiving the cards you've been dealt and doing your best to win with the hand you've got.

This journey of self-love, like all of Mind Strength, is a daily pursuit. A worthy one. One I'm still on. And when I drift, which I often do, I return to an affirmation that anchors me in this truth: *"I love and accept myself deeply and completely."*

Love the person you see in the mirror enough to be vulnerable, to put yourself out there, and to live with serenity—to accept the things you cannot change and to have the courage to change the things you can.

That's the real strength. That's Mind Strength.

THE PLAYBOOK

CLEAN THE SLATE

This Mind Strength exercise is inspired by the Al-Anon meetings I attended in 2020 during my "quarter-life crisis." Its foundation comes from Steps 8 and 9 of the 12 Steps.[9] The support I received from that program and the people in it became a cornerstone of who I am today and the work I do now.

1. **Take Inventory.** Write down the areas in your life where you haven't been fully honest—where you've lied, held back the truth, or worn a mask.

2. **Make It Right.** Choose one of those areas and make amends. Have the conversation. Own it. Set it straight.

3. ***Clear* It.** Forgive yourself for not being honest. Give yourself permission to let go, release the guilt, and stop carrying the weight you've been putting on yourself.

4. **Reflect.** Notice how much energy you gain when you stop carrying the mental burden.

Just think: **What would it look like to live unfiltered, free of stories, and to be fully, authentically you?**

Give yourself a clean slate—a fresh start—and make the conscious decision to code and anchor this skill: *"radical honesty," "tell the truth," "no stories,"* or *"honestly me."* Use it to lock in this mindset moving forward, to tell the truth and set yourself free from the mental weight, and to keep your inner environment clear and clean.

COACHING TIP

HURT VS. HARM

As a player, I had coaches who beat around the bush with me. I get it—when you're in that chair, it's hard to deliver hard news sometimes. But if you don't, you risk dragging the player along and causing more damage down the road.

That's where my guide came in: **Hurt vs. Harm**.

What you say might hurt in the moment—it might sting their feelings or cause discomfort. But if it's for their highest good and it won't harm them, then it's necessary to say. That's truth. That's honesty.

Use this as an example: It's like being in a relationship that's no longer working. By ending it, yes, there will be some hurt initially. But in the long run, you aren't harming that individual. On the other hand, if you stay and avoid making the change, you may avoid hurt in the moment, but you end up causing harm to both of you. And that harm brings far more damage and pain than hurt ever could.

This was Coach Leach to a T. Sure, some of the things he said hurt at times—but I always knew where he stood. By being honest with me, he didn't harm me in the process.

So use this as your gauge. Be honest. Will it hurt sometimes? Yes. But if it doesn't harm them, then it's the right thing to do.

Final Thought

What a tragedy it would be—to outwork everyone, beat the odds, and climb to the doorstep of your dreams... only to lose it all because you allowed the wrong voices, habits, lies, or distractions to sabotage your mindset. I've lived through that pain. I've seen what happens when you let your environment pull you down instead of lift you up.

Learn from my mistakes.

Do yourself a Mind Strength favor: Create and protect a winning environment—because as I've learned, Mind Strength isn't just about getting there... it's about staying there.

Chapter 7 Review —
Create and Sustain a Winning Environment

In this chapter, we got honest about the role your environment plays in sustaining success. Because getting to the top is only half the battle. Staying there? That takes discipline, clarity, and boundaries.

You can do all the right training. Stack your Mind Strength reps. Master your routines. But if your environment is toxic—if your circle drains more than it deposits—it will sabotage your progress. That's not theory. That's lived experience.

You learned how to:

- **Audit Your Core 5.** Identify the people you're spending the most time with and ask: Are they raising your standards or pulling you back?

- **Flip Peer Pressure.** Recognize the difference between negative and positive peer pressure, and use it to rise—not regress.

- **Set Boundaries That Stick.** Communicate clearly, follow through consistently, and protect your peace.

- **Evaluate Your Intake.** Be intentional about what you watch, read, listen to, and absorb. It's not entertainment—it's training.

- **Model What Works.** Find someone who's already done what you want to do, and apply their habits and mindset to your daily life.

- *Clear* **Your Inner Environment.** Tell the truth. Be vulnerable. Love yourself enough to risk rejection so you can live authentically as you.

Your mind is a high-performance machine. But even the best engine needs the right fuel and clean surroundings to run well.

Build the environment that matches your desires.

And protect it like your future depends on it—because it does.

CONCLUSION

"Easy, Easy"—A Mind Strength Audible

"Easy, easy."

That was the call I used at the line of scrimmage when it was time to change the play. The defense wasn't giving us the look we expected. The original call no longer fit. We had to pivot—quickly, calmly, deliberately. It didn't mean we were unprepared. It meant we were aware. We were present. We were ready.

That mindset—the willingness to audible—was one of the biggest reasons Coach Leach's quarterbacks were so effective. He gave us the freedom to adapt. He trusted us to think for ourselves, to lead, and to take ownership of what we were seeing on the field. That wasn't just football intelligence. That was life preparation.

Now, years later, "Easy, easy" has become something more. A mindset. A reset button. A call to pivot, not just in the pocket—but in life.

Because life doesn't always give you a clean read. The coverage changes. The blitz comes. The people around you yell the wrong things from the stands. You get hit. You fall. And when that happens, the play you'd planned is no longer enough. You need a new plan. You need presence. You need peace.

You need to call an audible.

I've had to do that many times in my own life. I've set goals, chased dreams, drawn up the perfect script—only to have life present me with something completely different. I've watched my best-laid plans fall apart. And I've had to stand there, take a breath, and call it:

"Easy, easy."

When I lost a job I'd been counting on.

When injuries disrupted my progress.

When relationships I valued came to an end.

When the pain felt personal and permanent.

I had to adjust. Not just what I was doing—but who I was being.

That's not weakness. That's Mind Strength. It's emotional agility. Mental resilience. The ability to stay grounded when the plan shifts and the pressure mounts. But sometimes even that isn't enough. Sometimes the audible you need isn't a new plan at all.

Sometimes the strongest thing you can do… is ask for help.

WHEN LIFE DOESN'T GO AS PLANNED

I've lived that. Many times.

There were moments in my life where everything seemed dialed in. The goals were clear.

The path made sense. The playbook was drawn up perfectly.

And then the defense shifted. The blitz came. Life hit me with something I didn't see coming. It's in those moments—the breakdowns, the pivots, the things you never would've chosen— where Mind Strength shows up the most. Because when your plan falls apart, you have two options.

You can panic.

Or you can pause.

You can white-knuckle your way through it and hope it holds.

Or you can take a breath, scan the field, and call the audible.

"Easy, easy."

WHAT THAT LOOKS LIKE IN REAL LIFE

Let's be clear—calling an audible isn't always glamorous. It's not a TED Talk moment.

Sometimes it feels messy. Raw. Uncertain. But that's when it matters most.

You lose the job you were banking on.

"*Easy, easy*"
You pivot. You recalibrate.
You find a better fit—one that aligns with who you really are.

A relationship ends.

"*Easy, easy*"
You stop outsourcing your identity.
You rebuild from the inside out. You rediscover peace.

You thought you'd be in the NFL for ten years—but you weren't.

"*Easy, easy*"
You shift focus. You find a deeper calling. You coach.
You write this book.

Sometimes even the strongest audible isn't about changing direction. It's about reaching out.

WHEN THE AUDIBLE IS ASKING FOR HELP

I still remember one of the hardest hits I ever took. My head was throbbing, pain radiating through my body. I tried to lift my helmet off the ground—but I couldn't. It was literally stuck in the grass at the old Qualcomm Stadium in San Diego. So I planted both hands, pushed hard, and ripped it out. A thick divot of turf came with it, clinging to my helmet like a warning.

That was a football hit. But it was nothing compared to the hits life would throw at me next.

Mind Strength is like learning how to change a tire before it blows. It prepares you for the unexpected. So when things go sideways—when you get a flat—you know how to pull over, fix it, and keep moving.

But what happens when all four tires blow at once?

What happens when the whole car catches fire?

That's what happened to me in 2019.

I was cut from the NFL for the fourth and final time.

My dad was diagnosed with cancer.

My mom was unraveling in a severe battle with her mental health.

My five-year relationship and engagement ended.

My dog died.

I'd undergone two hip surgeries.

And somewhere in all that loss, I lost myself.

I remember asking: *Who am I now?*

Life had knocked me flat—and this time, I didn't know how to get back up. So I reached out to my sister, Natalee. She heard it in my voice—the weight, the shakiness, the soul-level fatigue.

"Luke," she said. "You need help."

She gave me her therapist's number. And to her credit, she didn't just suggest it—she followed up to make sure I followed through.

I made the call.

And instantly, the shame crept in. I felt weak. I felt exposed. That old programming kicked in—rub some dirt on it, don't show emotion, tough it out.

I worried what people would think. My dad. My coaches. My teammates. I questioned what it said about my masculinity. My toughness. My identity.

But I showed up anyway. I walked into that office. I did the work. And looking back now, I can say this without hesitation:

It saved my life.

That season of therapy helped me reclaim who I was. It helped me find clarity, dignity, and peace. It didn't make me less of a man—it made me more of one. It made me stronger than I'd ever been.

Today therapy is a foundational part of my Mind Strength practice. Not because I'm broken, but because I want to stay whole. As Dr. Seuss wrote:

> *"And when you're in a Slump,*
> *you're not in for much fun.*
> *Un-slumping yourself*
> *is not easily done."*

Sometimes the most courageous audible you can call is this: "I need help." And the bravest thing you can do? Accept it.

THE FINAL WHISTLE

Mind Strength isn't about being perfect—it's about being present. It's not about being unbreakable, but about knowing how to rebuild when things fall apart. It doesn't mean you'll never face adversity; it means you'll know how to pivot when it comes. At its core, Mind Strength is about trusting yourself—your instincts, your preparation, your spirit—and having the courage to call the play that's right for you, no matter what the defense throws your way.

Two Roads, One Life

Let's finish where we started.

This great game of life we're playing—on the field, off the field—will either feel like Heaven or Hell. The good news is, we have the power to choose. No matter what life throws our way. No matter what mistakes we've made. No matter who's torn us down, what bad luck we've faced, or how long we've been stuck in failure.

None of that disqualifies you.

None of it removes your agency.

You still get to choose. And if you're ever unsure which road you're on, use this as your guide:

Hell is easy.
Heaven is hard.

Does the path ahead feel smooth, comfortable, popular?

Does it promise relief but deliver regret?

That's the easy road.

It's avoiding responsibility. Skipping workouts.

Letting your negative emotions lead.

Making excuses.

Reacting instead of preparing.

Blaming others when things don't go your way.

Living off approval.

Numbing out.

Letting your Inner Critic drive.

And most of all—refusing to ask for help, even when you know you need it.

That's Hell. It doesn't always look like fire—sometimes it just feels like emptiness.

And then there's the road that leads to Heaven.

It's quiet. Narrow. Often lonely.

It asks more of you than you think you have.

But if you stay on it, it gives back more than you could ever imagine.

It's showing up when you're tired.

Owning your mistakes.

Training your mind like it matters.

Forgiving people who didn't say sorry.

Saying no to things that steal your peace.

Staying in the fire long enough to be changed by it.

It's listening to the still, small voice inside you.

And having the courage to follow it.

Most people won't.

But you're not most people. You've been given the tools. You've done the work. You've called the audibles. And now, when life shifts again—and it will—you'll be ready. Because you know how to respond.

You know how to find your footing.

You know how to lead yourself.

So when the pressure rises, and it's time to choose—

You don't need to panic.

You don't need to prove anything.

Just breathe. Call it out. *"Easy, easy."*

Then take the road that costs more— and leads somewhere worth going.

ENDNOTES

1   Shyam Chaitanya et al., "Effect of Resonance Breathing on Heart Rate Variability and Cognitive Functions in Young Adults: A Randomised Controlled Study," *Cureus*, February 13, 2022, https://pmc.ncbi.nlm.nih.gov/articles/PMC8924557/.

2   By et al., "Fundamental Attribution Error Theory in Psychology," *Simply Psychology*, June 15, 2023, https://www.simplypsychology.org/fundamental-attribution.html.

3   Amrisha Vaish, Tobias Grossmann, and Amanda Woodward, "Not All Emotions Are Created Equal: The Negativity Bias in Social-Emotional Development.," *Psychological Bulletin* 134, no. 3 (May 2008): 383–403, https://doi.org/10.1037/0033-2909.134.3.383.

4   Roy F. Baumeister et al., "Bad Is Stronger Than Good," *Review of General Psychology* 5, no. 4 (2001): 323–370.

5   Tom Brady, Facebook post, April 10, 2018, https://www.facebook.com/TomBrady/posts/i-really-dont-like-leaving-much-up-to-fate-certainly-with-regard-to-my- football-/1763240550383754/.

6   Alan Baddeley et al., "Short-term memory is limited to about four 'chunks' of information," Short-term memory (Wikipedia, updated June 2025); citing Cowan, "magical number 4" capacity estimate.

7   Sean T. McGuire, "Bills' Josh Allen Reveals Pregame Playlist before Patriots, and It's Interesting," NESN.com, November 2, 2020, https://nesn.com/2020/11/bills-josh-allen-reveals-pregame-playlist-before-patriots-and-its-interesting/.

8   *Tom Brady Joins Colin Cowherd to Discuss Broadcast Prep, Belichick Days and Aaron Rodgers* | THE HERD, YouTube (The Herd with Colin Cowherd, 2024), https://www.youtube.com/watch?v=fwS7nlrUSZA.

9   "The Twelve Steps: Al-Anon Family Groups," Al, December 31, 2020, https://al-anon.org/for-members/the-legacies/the-twelve-steps/.

ABOUT LUKE FALK

Luke Falk is the all-time passing leader in Pac-12 history, a former NFL quarterback, and a former college football coach whose journey took him from walking on at Washington State University to becoming one of college football's most prolific passers. But his greatest transformation didn't happen under stadium lights—it happened in the space between his ears.

After navigating the pressures of elite competition, personal adversity, and the mental rollercoaster of high-performance sports, Luke discovered that the real edge isn't physical. It's mental.

Today, he's the founder of *Falk Mind Strength Coaching LLC*, a sought-after speaker, and a trusted Mind Strength coach to athletes, coaches, and high performers. Through his RLE (Real Life Experience) approach, Luke equips others with the tools to stay grounded under pressure, focused in chaos, and present in the moment—on and off the field.

Whether it's game day or a tough day, Luke's mission is simple: Help you master your mind so you can elevate your game—and your life.

Want Mind Strength Coaching? Learn more at coachlukefalk.com

ACKNOWLEDGMENTS

This book holds the fingerprints of *Wayne Dyer, John Wooden, Tony Robbins, Don Miguel Ruiz, Ed Mylett, Darren Hardy, Ryan Holiday, Dr. Stephen R. Covey, James Clear, Greg McKeown, Gay Hendricks, Napoleon Hill, Dale Carnegie, Robin Sharma, Zig Ziglar, Mike Leach, Bill Walsh, Dr. Craig Manning, Jon Gordon, Dave Ramsey, Dave Austin, Gary Mack, Dr. Henry Cloud, Dr. John Townsend, Al-Anon*, and many others. I have tried to honor and share the universal truths they have individually and collectively given voice to.

TO MY FAMILY

Foremost, I want to thank my beautiful, loving, and supportive wife, Meg. I believe one of the most important decisions you'll ever make is who you choose to spend your life with. So much of your success and the quality of your life is shaped by that relationship—and I definitely outkicked my coverage.

This journey over the last four years hasn't been easy as I've tried to find my footing post-playing career. I've bounced from job to job, idea to idea, and through it all, she has remained steady. She's given me the space to operate and has been everything—all at once. She's not only an amazing wife, but also the best mom to our family. Life is pretty incredible when your best friend is walking beside you. I love you Meg.

To my Charlotte girl… you are my everything. In the quiet hours of holding you, peace came over me, and clarity kicked in. I cherish those middle-of-the-night moments with you and the way you live completely in the moment. You inspire me daily. I love you more than love.

To my parents—There's no playbook for parenting—and now that I'm a father myself, I understand you both more clearly. You've always done what you believed was best to give me opportunities and a better life than you had. I'm deeply grateful for the love, the lessons, and the countless sacrifices. I'm thankful for all of it—the highs and the lows. It shaped the man I've become. Without you two, none of this happens.

Mom, at your core — the true essence of who you are — you are as pure and good as anyone I've ever known. I love you so much, and I wish you nothing but happiness and peace. Love, your bud. Peas and carrots.

Dad, I've told you this many times. I once heard Ed Mylett talk about "the one"—the person who changes the family trajectory. That's you. You came from nothing and used your own mind strength to put our family on a better path. Many of the Mind Strength principles I coach today were first taught to me by you — long before I had the words to describe them. Your influence runs deep, and I carry it with me every day. I love you, Pops.

To my sister Natalee—You are one of my best friends, and your role in this book can't be overstated. You've been there for every step of this journey—from being my accountability partner during the book proposal and writing process to encouraging me through the highs and lows. You're one of the closest people in my life and someone I'll always want in my Core 5.

To my sister Shea—growing up, it felt like I had another protector. You always looked out for me, not just physically but, more importantly, emotionally. I've always felt your support, and I still do today. You've been one of my biggest cheerleaders, and your belief in me has meant more than you'll ever know.

To my in-laws—I certainly lucked out with you both. I'm grateful for your love, support, and for raising such an incredible woman in Meg. I love you and appreciate you deeply.

TO MY BOOK TEAM

Scott Miller—without you, this book wouldn't exist. You're the best in the business, and your energy is contagious. You built an all-star team around me and helped bring my vision to life. Your ability to deliver tough feedback without putting up walls is a gift we'd all benefit from.

Platte & Kennidy Clark—you turned this book into gold! Your editing insights and overall process helped me articulate and elevate the message I've held inside for years. You've been the perfect teammates to bring this to life.

Davin Salvagno—your guidance and mentorship throughout the process were invaluable. From book strategy to coaching insights to honest feedback, you've been incredibly generous and impactful.

Kaleb and Nikki — You both have a unique gift for enhancing and elevating a message—and your contributions helped bring clarity, color, and resonance to this project.

Mel Wise—the design elements you created for this book truly were the icing on the cake. Thank you for your amazing and gifted work.

TO MY COACHES

Mike Favero and Logan Brown—You two embody why sports and coaching matter: because of the relationships and the impact. Your influence on me runs deep.

Mike Leach—what can I say? None of this happens without you. You gave me a shot when a hundred others didn't. You stayed true to your word and built an environment where I could thrive. Your wisdom—simple yet profound—was all over this book. I regret not seeing it sooner. Losing you felt like losing a father figure I hadn't said everything to. Thank you, Coach. Your fingerprints are all over these pages.

Eric Mele—you were the one who found me in Logan, Utah. You took a chance when most didn't even watch my tape. You got me my shot, and I'll always be grateful.

Janice Erickson—Words can't describe the impact you've had on me. Thank you for teaching me one of the most powerful tools in my belt—clearing. Before every game, major event, or turbulent moment in life, you've been a steady presence and there every step of the way.

Dr. Karin Marin—You are living proof that God sends the right people into our lives at the right time. The therapy work we've done together has been life-changing—not just for me, but for my family. Your guidance has been invaluable, and I'll be forever thankful.

Wayne Dyer—I never had the chance to meet you, but I feel like I know you. You were the one who started me on my Mind Strength journey. In 2015, I called my dad and said, "I know what I want to do with my life." Instead of staying on the phone, he flew up the next day, and over lunch I told him, "Dad, I want to do what Wayne Dyer does—I want to write, speak, and help people be the best versions of themselves." That seed you planted has taken root, and just like the alchemist's journey, I now find myself living that vision. Thank you.

Dr. Craig Manning —You've been a major pillar in my Mind Strength journey. Before our work together, I was an unconfident kid who didn't believe in himself. You helped change my belief system, and the principles and sessions we shared are still ingrained in my mindset today. I'm grateful beyond words.

To the many other coaches who've impacted me—there are too many to list, but I hope you know how much you're appreciated.

TO MY TEAMMATES

When I think about my playing days, it's not the wins or the crowds I miss the most—it's you. The in-between moments. The relationships. Especially those early WSU days. You'll always have my respect. I do have regrets: that later in my career I didn't bring the same intentionality to those relationships. It wasn't about performance—it was about presence. But every part has shaped me. Thank you for being part of my story.

Nick Begg—In 2020, the foundation of this book was built. Those nights after work in your Newport condo, where we sat down and hashed out ideas for a Mind Strength curriculum, were foundational. You helped get the ball rolling, and those early conversations played a key role in bringing this book to life.

TO MY READER FEEDBACK GROUP

You know who you are. Your honest feedback and thoughtful insights helped shape the messaging and refine the flow of this book. I'm honored to share something I'm truly proud of—and you were a key part of making that possible.

TO MY CLIENTS

Thank you for your intention and your dedication. You're the reason I get to live out my dream and purpose as a coach.

TO THE READERS

Thank you for picking up this book. My life's mission is to help people unlock their full potential through strengthening their minds. I believe we all have untapped greatness—and when we train our minds to be a source of power instead of interference, we begin to access it. I hope this book has helped you begin that journey.

It is a journey—not a destination.

Enjoy the ride.

—*COACH LUKE FALK*

CONTINUE YOUR MIND STRENGTH JOURNEY

If this book resonated with you, the next step is simple: **apply what you've learned.**

Coach Luke Falk works with athletes, teams, and leaders to help them **master their mind and elevate their game**—whether that game is sports, business, or life.

Through his Mind Strength Coaching services, Luke offers:

- On-demand Mind Strength programs
- Live and virtual Mind Strength speaking engagements
- Team and organizational Mind Strength training
- Select one-on-one Mind Strength coaching

 To explore current programs, coaching opportunities, or to learn how Mind Strength training can support you, your athlete, or your organization, visit: **coachlukefalk.com**.

Follow Coach Luke Falk on the following platforms:

 @coachlukefalk    @coachlukefalk    Coach Luke Falk

BOOK LUKE FALK

TO SPEAK WITH YOUR TEAM,
PROGRAM, OR ORGANIZATION

Luke is represented by the Gray+Miller Agency, a leading speaking bureau comprised of the world's most diverse, engaging, and influential speakers, authors, and thought leaders.

For speaking inquiries please visit **graymilleragency.com** or submit a request at **coachlukefalk.com**.

Maison Vero

Representing a community of authors whose books have collectively sold hundreds of millions of copies, the founders of The Gray + Miller Agency launched Maison Vero, a professional publishing house that partners with rising authors to bring their thought leadership to the world. Our representation covers every aspect of thought leadership, including U.S. senators, governors, and ambassadors, billionaire founders and entrepreneurs, researchers, academics, scientists, consultants, practitioners, social influencers, C-suite leaders, adventurers, professional athletes, artists, and creators. We partner with thought leaders and world changers like you who have a story to tell. By bringing decades of professional expertise to our clients, we are charting a new path in a timeless industry that transcends publishing norms, transforming powerful thoughts into impactful books that inspire minds, ignite hearts, and open doors.

Visit **maisonvero.com** to view our growing list of authors, or to submit a proposal for publication consideration.

Follow Maison Vero for insight and inspiration on social media:

in MaisonVero **f** MaisonVero **◎** MaisonVero MaisonVeroPublishing

For information about special discounts for bulk purchases, please call 1-949-333-4872 or email info@graymilleragency.com.

Maison Vero is a partner brand of The Gray + Miller Agency, a speaking, literary, and talent consortium. For more information on the talent represented by The Gray + Miller Agency, or to bring any of our thought leaders to your organization or live event, please visit our website at **graymilleragency.com**.